From Ship to Shuttle

NASA Orbiter-Naming Program

September 1988-May 1989

Front cover:
(Top) **Endeavour** *by Paul Phillips. Courtesy of The Natural History Museum, London.*

(Bottom) The Space Shuttle orbiter **Endeavour** *officially rolls out of the Rockwell International facility, Palmdale, California, April 25, 1991. NASA photo.*

Title:
From Ship to Shuttle, *a title of several Orbiter-Naming entries, was first suggested to us by the third grade class,* **City Park School, Monticello, Arkansas.**

*Model of His Majesty's Bark
Endeavour. Courtesy of
National Maritime Museum,
Greenwich, London.*

FROM SHIP TO SHUTTLE

NASA Orbiter-Naming Program
September 1988-May 1989

Elementary and Secondary Branch

Education Division

Office of Human Resources and Education

NASA Headquarters

October 1991

EP-276

Foreword

BY CONGRESSIONAL ACTION IN 1987, the National Aeronautics and Space Administration (NASA) was authorized to provide an opportunity for American school students to name the new Space Shuttle orbiter being built to replace the *Challenger*. The Council of Chief State School Officers (CCSSO), an education organization representing the chief education officials of the nation, was asked by NASA to assist in the development and administration of this exciting and important educational activity.

The state commissioners and superintendents of education were pleased to join several other educators and our colleagues at NASA in planning an educational program that would result in selecting the most suitable name for the new orbiter. The NASA Orbiter-Naming Program was a challenge to American students that stimulated study and research. Students were required to work in teams and to integrate knowledge by connecting historical, scientific, technical, and artistic information in a persuasive case supporting their recommendation. It was a program that would leave a legacy of inquiry in our nation's classrooms.

The NASA Orbiter-Naming Program was launched in March 1988, and its success is evidenced by the enormous interest generated both nationally and internationally. The CCSSO distributed more than 490,000 Announcements of Opportunity to participate in the program. Students enrolled in United States public and private schools, elementary through secondary (kindergarten-grade 12), were eligible to participate. Qualifying schools included schools in the 50 states, the District of Columbia, the five U.S. jurisdictions (American Samoa, Guam, Puerto Rico, the Northern Mariana Islands, and the Virgin Islands), Bureau of Indian Affairs schools, Department of Defense Dependent Schools, and Department of State overseas schools.

In response to requests from teachers, 68,690 Program Entry Packets were distributed. Teams involving a total of 71,652 students returned 6,154 entry packets to the council for processing. The total number of Division 1 entries (kindergarten-grade 6) was 4,059 and for Division 2 (grades 7-12), there were 2,095 entries. Of the total entries, 3,834 were from elementary schools, 1,109 from middle schools, 673 from junior high schools, and 538 from senior high schools. The teams, which numbered from 4 to 888 members each, submitted 422 different names.

The council is delighted that American students met this challenge so well and commends the U.S. Congress and NASA for providing them with this opportunity. We are proud to have been part of this educational program.

Gordon M. Ambach
Executive Director
Council of Chief State School Officers

Preface

FROM *SHIP TO SHUTTLE* presents to teachers a selection of interdisciplinary activities related to the Space Shuttle that were designed by students for the NASA Orbiter-Naming Program.

The program had two entry divisions. Division 1 included students from kindergarten through 6th grade, and Division 2 included students, 7th through 12th grade. To enter the competition, students had to form teams with an adult team coordinator who had to be a member of the school faculty.

Each entry was reviewed at three levels. Level 1 consisted of a screening by the Council of Chief State School Officers, who reviewed the entries and forwarded those qualified to a state-level coordinator. At Level II, a board convened by the coordinator judged the entries. The state-level review boards announced one winner in each division of their competitions in March 1989, and forwarded 111 entries to NASA for selection of the national winners. At Level III, two NASA committees—one for the names and one for the projects—judged the state-level winners and forwarded the results to the NASA Administrator.

This book contains a selection of 39 state-level winners to offer teachers a variety of space-related classroom activities from which they may adapt an idea, a portion of a project, or a research topic for interested students, a class, an aerospace unit, or a team activity with another classroom. The organization of the book follows that of the competition. There are two parts: Division 1 and Division 2. In each division, the national winner's project is first, followed by other projects listed in alphabetical order by state, and a bibliography compiled from suggestions by the state-level winning teams.

The 39 activities chosen for the book represent the breadth and scope of the Orbiter-Naming Program. They are from all grades, K-12; public schools and private academies; Gifted and Talented and special education classes; metropolitan areas and small towns; teams from one class or several classes; small teams from one grade and large teams from several grades.

Part I of the entry packets identified the team's coordinator and student members. Where a coordinator added the name of an assistant or co-worker, the first name was designated the single team coordinator permitted by the competition. The activities in this book include the coordinator's and team members' names unless the team's number made a listing prohibitive. Addresses also are included, so interest in particular projects may be pursued further.

Because space is limited, the activities in the book are synopses of the teams' projects and include the three major elements in the Program Entry Packets:

- *The Name.* The first section of each activity is the name proposed by the team and their statement on why they chose it. Their compositions are quoted in the book, with lengthy explanations edited or paraphrased. (Part II of the entry packet.) *The typeface and composition of this section are modified to distinguish these quoted parts from the descriptions of the students' projects.*

- *The Project.* This section of the activity bears the title the students gave their project or a title that describes it. It is a compilation of the team's explanation of their project and a description of their research written by the team coordinator with the students. (Parts III and IV of the entry packet.)

- *Model for the Future.* This is the final statement in each entry, the team's suggestion for continuing or expanding the project in the class, school, or community. (Part IV of the entry packet.)

Endeavour was the most-often suggested name (1,016) and accounted for almost one-third of the state-level winners. It also appears more often than any other name in this book.

The individual entries are illustrated with the ship whose name was recommended, a portrait of the ship's captain, or an object relevant to the ship's voyage. The illustrations are as varied as the ships, historically significant not only as representations of the sea vessels themselves but of the times in which the pictures were created. It is hoped that by representing a variety of artistic media—prints, paintings, sketches, models, photographs—and a wide range of styles, the illustrations not only will enhance the rationale for the selection of ships, but also may inspire further study of the arts and humanities, their place in different times and different cultures, as well as their relationships with science and technology.

Appendices list the Council of Chief State School Officers, state department coordinators, state-level winners, and names of the ships suggested, and provide information on the two *Endeavours*.

NASA appreciated the opportunity to work with Mr. Gordon M. Ambach, Executive Director of CCSSO, and his staff and wishes to thank the hundreds of teachers, administrators, and other educators who served as judges for the selection of the state-level winners.

We are grateful to the National Maritime Museum, Greenwich, London, and to the other museums, associations, and organizations who provided information and illustrations for this book, as well as to numerous teachers in the United States and the United Kingdom and to the Mystic Seaport Museum and the Yale Center for British Art, Connecticut, for their assistance in researching and obtaining photographs.

Robert W. Brown, Ph.D.
Deputy Associate Administrator for Human Resources and Education
NASA Headquarters

Contents

DIVISION 1   Kindergarten–Grade 6

DIVISION 2   Grades 7-12

Appendices

The Orbiter-Naming Program

Sarah Alford of the Division 1 national winning team from Senatobia Middle School, Mississippi, receives the team award from President Bush. Joining in the applause are astronauts from Shuttle Mission STS-30. Photo by Michael Sargent, The White House.

On behalf of the Division 2 national winning team from Tallulah Falls School, Inc., Georgia, May Chan receives the team award from President Bush. Looking on are the Atlantis crew—(from left to right) Mission Specialists Mary Cleave and Mark Lee, Pilot Ronald Grabe, Mission Specialist Norman Thagard, and Commander David Walker. Photo by David Valdez, The White House.

Introduction

ON MARCH 10, 1986, House Joint Resolution 559 introduced by Congressman Tom Lewis (R-FL) established the NASA Orbiter-Naming Program. The legislation called for the replacement orbiter to be named by students in response to the outpouring of concerns by youngsters after the *Challenger* accident. In October 1987, Congress authorized a program for a name to be selected "from among suggestions submitted by students in elementary and secondary schools."

The Education Division at NASA Headquarters accepted responsibility for developing a national outreach program that offered American students the opportunity to name Orbiter Vehicle (OV) 105, the replacement Space Shuttle orbiter. The Elementary and Secondary Branch of the Division designed and conducted the orbiter-naming competition to enhance students' interest in and enthusiasm for space exploration through educational research related to exploration, discovery, or experimentation.

The orbiter-naming competition had two components: the name suggested and a project. NASA's first orbiters were named after sea vessels used in research and exploration, and that tradition was to be continued with OV-105. Thus, the new name also had to be the name of an exploratory or research sea vessel, be appropriate for a spacecraft and capture the spirit of America's mission in space, and be a name easy to pronounce for radio transmission. In honor of the 51-L mission crew, the name *Challenger* was retired.

The related classroom projects prepared by student teams had to: (1) support and justify the name selected; (2) be interdisciplinary; and (3) be creative and innovative. Each entry included a list of the learning goals of the project and a description of how the project fit the curriculum objectives of the school system, its educational value for the students participating in the project, and the project's potential as a model for future classroom and school activities.

We are all aware of how exciting and stimulating space exploration is to young people. They accept it as part of their lives and look to it for their future. The Orbiter-Naming Program gave students and their teachers an active role in NASA's space flight program and, at the same time, opened new avenues of interest in all aspects of space exploration. It stimulated their learning in the arts and humanities as well as in science, mathematics, and technology. It encouraged involvement by parents and the community. And it required teamwork, decision-making, and problem-solving.

NASA invited the Council of Chief State School Officers with its national network to all states, jurisdictions, and agencies to administer the program. The goal was to reach every school, offer each class a chance to participate, and spark the imagination of individual young minds. Final participation included the 50 states, District of Columbia, four of the five U.S. jurisdictions, Bureau of Indian Affairs schools, Department of Defense Dependent Schools, and Department of State schools. A coordinator was appointed for each state-level program to organize judging for the competition and attendant activities.

The state-level competitions resulted in 111 winning projects. Within their respective geographic areas, the NASA Center Educational Programs Officers recognized the student teams, their coordinators, and their schools. The special recognition ranged from certificates and appropriate mementos to on-center programs and school visits by the NASA aerospace education specialists.

The 111 projects chosen for national consideration presented a delightful variety of both names and projects. In May 1989, President George Bush selected and announced the winning name—*Endeavour*—based upon recommendations by the NASA Admininstrator. The name was suggested by the winning teams of both divisions—Senatobia Middle School, Senatobia, Mississippi, in Division 1, and Tallulah Falls School Inc., Tallulah Falls, Georgia, in Division 2.

The teams were awarded a trip to Washington, D.C., where they received an invitation to the White House. Referring to them as leaders of tomorrow, President Bush saluted the national winners at a White House ceremony. The President said that in winning the competition, the teams "showed how the possibilities of tomorrow point us onward and upward. . . . Both of your schools chose the name *Endeavour,* which Webster's defines as 'to make an effort, strive, to try to reach or achieve.' And each of your schools has lived that definition."

At the same program, the President also recognized the crew of the Space Shuttle *Atlantis,* who had successfully deployed the *Magellan* spacecraft during their STS-30 mission earlier in the month. The President noted that the celebration was for two space programs that reflect America's continuity. "For in *Atlantis'* deployment of *Magellan,* we salute achievement which has come to pass; and in *Endeavour,* the glory which still lies ahead."

At the conclusion of his remarks, the President presented a plaque to each national winning team.

The winners' Washington visit included a reception in their honor at the National Air and Space Museum. Admiral Richard H. Truly, NASA Administrator, presented a plaque to each student and team coordinator. Congressman Lewis, whose legislation had created the Orbiter-Naming Program, also addressed the group.

In addition to the splendid fact that OV-105 always will be known by the name they suggested and their award-trip to the Nation's capital, the teams enjoyed a two-day School Involvement Program conducted by the Elementary and Secondary Branch at their schools. Special events honored the students, their team coordinators, and the faculties, parents, and community members who guided and assisted their orbiter-naming projects.

In Senatobia, astronaut Dr. Linda M. Godwin, a member of the STS-37 mission that would launch the *Gamma Ray Observatory* in April 1991, joined NASA educational personnel in presenting programs for students in every grade as well as at a community reception honoring all participants. In Tallulah Falls, NASA lecturers and astronaut Dr. Manley L. "Sonny" Carter, Jr., a member of the STS-33 crew who flew in November 1989, met with the entire student body, as well as with individual classes, and also presented a program for the community.

Members of the national winning teams were present for the *Endeavour* rollout ceremony on April 25, 1991, when Rockwell International delivered the new orbiter to NASA at its facilities in Palmdale, California. Earlier that month, the Tallulah Falls team and the Education Division staff were deeply saddened by the death of astronaut Sonny Carter who was killed in an airplane accident. In his memory, at the rollout each Georgia student wore the STS-33 crew patch.

This publication, *From Ship to Shuttle,* is the summary project of the Orbiter-Naming Program. NASA's Education Division considers the entries included to be useful for both teachers and leaders of youth groups. We hope that just as each team has left a legacy for the next class and for its school, so will its activities be a springboard for many other teachers who share them through this volume.

The Orbiter-Naming Program was an especially rewarding experience. We have been gratified by the enthusiastic response to the challenges of the program and pleased by the variety and quality of the projects. In the proposals submitted from throughout the nation in addition to those included in this book, the participants provided evidence of their excitement with the program. There were students fascinated with local history and others intrigued with interplanetary travel; some cafeteria staffs honored their students' projects with special "space menus" that included Space Spaghetti Sauce over NASA Noodles, Planet Peas, and Rocket Rolls, and others who saved egg cartons and packing materials that became computers, satellites, and TV monitors; there was a class whose birthday party for Captain Cook included a cake decorated with LIFESAVERS and limeade in honor of the vitamin C in the *Endeavour* crew's diet that helped defeat scurvy.

There was the fifth-grade class who wrote a book and dedicated it to the kindergarten class with the command that they review the predictions when they become fifth-graders themselves. Then they were to continue the tradition by making their own space predictions for the kindergarten class of that year.

Students enjoyed rap writing, designed comic books and an alphabet book using words connected with Captain Cook and *Endeavour,* invented word games and puzzles, and created logos and T-shirts; they learned the techniques of conducting surveys and of interviewing; they tested the names they chose in random public polls and used CBs, walkie-talkies, and school intercoms to test the clarity for radio transmission. They visited science centers and toured ships, enjoyed visits to museums and created their own museums in the classroom, and designed models of their sea vessels as well as spaceships.

They learned technical skills involving tools, cameras, audiovisual equipment, and computers. They were surprised to learn "a greater load of information" in a variety of subjects and to discover that aerospace careers cover a wide range of occupations. They saw role models in the scientists and technicians who work together to make the orbiter a reality. And they learned that working as a team was more efficient, more productive, and more fun than fighting over who should be first or which job was most important.

The students thanked their parents for their concern and involvement, for chauffeuring them to after-school and Saturday meetings, to museums and on field trips; for sewing costumes and creating props; for offering critiques and serving as subjects for polls. They also were grateful to teachers who stayed late, listened to their ideas, and guided their efforts; to librarians who introduced them to the complexities of research and taught them reference skills so that they "learned to do better looking up things in books like encyclopedias"; and to principals who waited until the last child got a ride home, provided supplies, and sometimes came up with "a little financing."

They appreciated people in their communities—the local businesses that sponsored and encouraged their efforts and the interior decorator who advised on colors for a game board; fire and police departments who provided equipment; the media who publicized their projects; and college and university professors and students who listened, offered feedback, and lent facilities.

There were two especially rewarding results. One was the almost unanimous expression by the teams that learning should be fun. The second was the number of students who discovered the profession of teaching—its difficulties, pleasures, and the knowledge that it is <u>hard work</u>.

Two enthusiastic statements also indicated that the program enjoyed success on all levels. One exuberant third-grader told the teacher, ". . . even if our name is not picked, we are still winners! Just look at what all we have learned." And a team coordinator suggested that NASA should allow the children of America to name all their major projects and listed "New thematic units for NASA: Name the New Planetary Probe, Name the New Solar Probe, Name the New Orbiting Satellite, Name the New Launch Vehicle, etc."

Endeavour is scheduled for its first voyage in spring 1992. In addressing the *Atlantis* crew and the students at the White House, President Bush thanked them, saying, "For you've acted not for us alone, but for generations to come. And in so doing, you're making possible, now and tomorrow, that picture of the orbiter lifting off; its rise a swirl of magic; and of Americans cheering its safety and success and dreaming of the new worlds and faraway heavens, which form America's destiny."

When *Endeavour* lifts off, every student, every team coordinator, parent, and community who participated in the Orbiter-Naming Program should feel a special pride and excitement, knowing they shared in its naming.

DIVISION 1

Kindergarten–Grade 6

Endeavour

Endeavour *model showing crew and stores positioned within. Courtesy of National Maritime Museum, Greenwich, London.*

Why *Endeavour*

SENATOBIA MIDDLE SCHOOL
303 College Street
Senatobia, Mississippi 38668

NATIONAL WINNER

Martha S. Riales
Team Coordinator
Gifted Education Teacher
Grades 3-6

TEAM MEMBERS
GRADE 5

Sarah Alford
Thomas Anzalone
Ryan Burke
Casey Craig
Melody Durrett
Jennifer Hale
Spencer Miller
Mac Monteith
Zack Zettergren

The Gifted Education Class, Grade 5, at the Senatobia Middle School proposes the name *Endeavour* for the OV 105 because of the following reasons:

1 The word "endeavor" as defined in *Webster's New Collegiate Dictionary,* 1977, means:

   a. to strive, achieve, or reach
   b. to attempt by exerting effort
   c. to work with a set purpose
   d. a serious determined effort

The United States Space Shuttle Program's mission spirit is a united effort to strive, reach, and achieve goals in areas of exploration and discovery. NASA personnel work with the set purpose of utilizing space for experimentation as the NASA team works together with a serious determined effort to make the space program profitable for establishing international peace boundaries, for improvement of medical technology, and to provide for a national defense.

2 The *Endeavour* was a sea vessel commanded by Lieutenant James Cook in 1769-71. Lt. Cook, a seaman and scientist, was sent to Tahiti in the South Pacific to observe and record the important and seldom occurring event of the planet Venus passing between the earth and the sun. Tahiti was the best location for the view of this event just as positions in space are best for viewing today's activities of our galaxy. The satellites left in space by our space shuttles make it possible for us to study and explore areas in space unknown to mankind.

3 The payload of the *Endeavour* consisted of medicine, scientific equipment, and trinkets for trading. The payload of the space shuttle is similar. Commercial contracts include privately owned product experimentation and satellites.

4 The *Endeavour's* captain was responsible for preventing scurvy, a common sailor's illness, by providing specific food supplies on the voyage. Special care has been made for providing adequate food and vitamin supplies, exercise, and medication for the astronauts on space missions . . . .

5 The *Endeavour* was well equipped for its mission of exploration and experimentation. Its passengers included a botanist, a naturalist, a scientist commander, two artists, and two animals. Specimens of plant and animal life were collected and examined. Observations were made and recorded. Likewise, the shuttle missions include persons of various professions based on the type of exploration or experimentation assignment. Animals have been included on some space missions.

6 Just as the shuttle was sent on a secret military mission, the *Endeavour* was given a secret assignment. It was commissioned to explore the new land believed to be located in the Southern Hemisphere called Terra Australis.

7 The *Endeavour* successfully overcame many dangerous difficulties to prevent it from being destroyed. The spirit of America's space mission is to overcome the tragedy of the *Challenger*.

8 The word *Endeavour* is easily received and comprehended when sent via a public address system. There would be no problem using the name, *Endeavour*, when communicating with astronauts on shuttle missions.

9 *Endeavour* is not an uncommon name; however, it is a name sophisticated enough to represent the spirit of the United States of America's mission in space.

First Endeavours in Space

The project, *First Endeavours in Space*, a hands-on activity created by the fifth grade Gifted and Talented class, was designed to teach the lower elementary students facts about the space program and to involve them in active participation via a simulated space camp. The project was planned by the group and their coordinator, with individual team members assuming responsibility as captains for single areas of activity within the camp.

The Space Camp Simulation was set up in the school gymnasium. For their nine activities, the students constructed a space bubble, space suit, sleeping bag, Shuttle models, games, and experiments to use in their presentations. They collected space food and walkie-talkies, borrowed a manipulator arm, constructed posters, labeled diagrams, and practiced their speeches. The nine areas were:

■ *Space Shuttle Simulator*—Pupils entered a space bubble to learn about the parts of the Space Shuttle and to experience the feeling of enclosure in it.

■ *Space Clothing*—Participants tried on a space suit simulation.

■ *Medicine and Space*—Participants were blindfolded and turned around in a swivel chair to experience dizziness, a common space-related illness.

■ *Space Food*—Students were given samples of freeze-dried space food.

■ *Space Structures*—Participants built a space structure from plastic straws.

■ *Sleep and Exercise in Space*—The youngsters experienced sleeping standing up and were told about the importance of exercise in space.

■ *Payload Packaging*—Teams of pupils packaged an egg "payload" and dropped it from the gym window to see the importance of payload packaging.

- *Space Communications*—Students used walkie-talkies to experience wireless communication, were given a demonstration of the computer as a means of communicating, and learned about communication satellites.

- *Work in Space*—Students had a hands-on experience using a manipulator arm for transporting objects.

Kindergarten, first-grade, and second-grade students and teachers were brought to the gym by grades. Divided into small groups, the children rotated to a different area every 10 minutes. In each area the students listened to the captain's talk as he or she explained and demonstrated the subject. Then the pupils experienced a related activity. Upon completion of all nine areas, participants went to an evaluation area where they used electric boards, designed and constructed to give them immediate feedback on the degree of learning acquired in each area.

The team captains designed coloring books using their OV-105 name and the activities of the space camp simulation to give to the visiting students as a tangible remembrance of their "First Endeavours in Space."

Among several additional related activities, the team took a trip to the Alabama Space and Rocket Center, Huntsville, and visited NASA's Marshall Space Flight Center to learn more about space projects.

Model for the Future

This project can be adapted to any grade level, but is most effective for use with pupils who wish to interact with younger students. It gives students a purpose for acquiring knowledge (to be able to teach) and to use the knowledge on a high cognitive level. The project may be used as a whole or in part, and can be adapted for use in any classroom.

Endeavour

A view of the Endeavour River with *Endeavour* beached for repairs, June 1770. *Engraving by Will Byrne, probably after a drawing by Sydney Parkinson. Courtesy of National Maritime Museum, Greenwich, London.*

Why *Endeavour*

FOUR PEAKS SCHOOL
17300 Calaveras Street
Fountain Hills, Arizona 85268

Cathleen A. Brown
Team Coordinator
Gifted Class Instructor
Grades 1-6
Language Arts, Mathematics,
Independent Study

TEAM MEMBERS
GRADE 6

Jacob Altizer
Mike Bachman
Chris Erickson
Kayli Fleischman
Anthony Germinaro
Tisha Henes
Stephanie Kimber
Ami Kuisle
Jason Meador
Trygve Ulrickson
Staci Underwood
Michael Ware
Kevin Womble

The sea vessel after which we found our title was an exploration ship captained by the famous James Cook. He captained maybe one of the greatest sea vessels of all time. He ventured on an important expedition in the history of exploration. He sailed to Tahiti to observe the transit of Venus. From Tahiti, he traveled to the South Pacific on an expedition for the British Royal Society to prove the existence of Antarctica. Unfortunately, they did not discover the great continent, but they made an interesting find on their way home.

They discovered New Zealand, where they were attacked by Aborigines, and were forced to evacuate the premises; then they sailed around the eastern coast of Australia, where they were caught on the Great Barrier Reef. Cook thought about his crew; "How could I get them to safety?" He decided to jettison some of his cargo, and when the ship floated to the surface they noticed a huge gash in the hull of their vessel. The crew paddled to the shore and repaired the hole. It took a month; one year later he sailed home.

Endeavour captures America's space program because endeavour means to try, and that is what America's space program is doing. Our great country is rebounding from the *Challenger* disaster of nearly three years ago. We need to fix our space program just as Cook fixed his ship when he and his crew were caught up on the Great Barrier Reef in Australia.

The name *Endeavour* is appropriate for OV 105 because it is a sea vessel. Secondly, it applies to the rules set by NASA because it was used for exploration and research. Lastly, we feel that the *Endeavour* is the best name for the new orbiter because it captures the spirit of the American space program by reflecting the positive feelings the public has about the rejuvenation of our space program.

6 & 1/2 Hours

The team's objective was to create a project that would be both informative and entertaining. They decided to write and film a newscast and, deriving the name from *48 Hours,* they called their program *6 & 1/2 Hours,* because they were in school six and one-half hours each day.

They wanted their newscast to reflect all their research into NASA and sea exploration and their observations as "aware" students. Their project began with researching names of ships. After narrowing their list to James Cook and Sir Walter Raleigh and their voyages, they staged a debate between Raleigh's *Destiny* and Cook's *Endeavour.* *Endeavour* proved to be the best title for OV-105. The next step was to create their news program. The outline:

I. Credits

II. Opening
   A. Personal introduction from anchor persons
   B. Preview of what newscast contains

III. Interviews
   A. General background of name
   B. James Cook and crew
   C. Royal Society

IV. Commercial Break
   A. So long from anchor persons
   B. NASA commercial
   C. Kitty-Kraut (sauerkraut cat food) commercial

V. Interviews
   A. Anchor persons
   B. NASA space engineer/scientist
   C. NASA official

VI. Commercial
   A. So long from anchor persons
   B. Space-Tuff pants commercial

VII. Closing
   A. Person on the street
   B. Closing from anchor persons
   C. Credits

Sections of the outline were assigned to small groups of students for writing the script. Each section of the script was submitted to the class for evaluation and revision. Upon completion of the script, they planned the filming. First, they assigned parts to each member of the team. Then they created backdrops, and, with assistance from parents, made costumes and obtained props. Next, they memorized their parts, formed teams to film each portion of the video, and learned how to operate the video camera. Then they filmed their project.

In evaluating the project, the team found many good points and some areas they wished they could redo. They felt a real sense of commitment to the orbiter name they selected. Whether or not they won, they hoped *Endeavour* would be the new name. One area that they wanted to improve in was learning how to videotape and how to edit. The technical aspects of their project were often frustrating for them.

Model for the Future

The team hopes the project can become part of the regular sixth-grade gifted curriculum. Although they realize that future classes most likely will not have a contest to enter, the students see how certain parts of their project could be used again and again: learning how to evaluate, using the debate process to choose a victor, and the idea of teamwork. This activity gave them the opportunity to work together. They see teamwork as an important life skill and believe it should be part of the curriculum.

Adventure

The *Resolution* and *Adventure* in Matavai Bay, Tahiti, *by William Hodges. Courtesy of National Maritime Museum, Greenwich, London.*

Why *Adventure*

MESA VIEW SCHOOL
17601 Avilla Lane
Huntington Beach,
California 92647

Scott Stark
Team Coordinator
Teacher, Grade 6

TEAM MEMBERS

Truman Chen
Karen Dawes
John Gordon
Jennifer Knox
Hillery Martin
Kenna Masuda
Dan Orris
Ben Price
Tracy Sandie
Teresa Velarde
Eric Wershing
Jason Williams

The Mesa View School team listed several reasons for their choice of the name *Adventure*. First, it describes both the spirit of the founders of the United States who saw the continent as the land of opportunity and of the nation's space program, which also offers opportunities; it describes the essence of the space program—man's interest in and desire to know and understand the universe and himself; and it is a word that means "to seek new places and ideas," gives thought to the future, and creates the idea of excitement.

In 1772, Captain James Cook set forth on his second adventure to the uncharted seas of the South Pacific with two ships, *Resolution* and *Adventure*. He took the most modern equipment of his time and a crew that included astronomers, scientists, and artists to record new discoveries and to refine the means of determining longitude. Cook's expedition ventured into the high southern latitudes, bearing south and west where the ocean had not been traced by man before, and crossed the Antarctic Circle for the first time in history. They discovered new islands, where Cook put ashore some animals he had brought along with him. *Adventure* went on to become the first English ship to circumnavigate the globe from west to east. The ship also took aboard an islander, Omai, from Huahme, and took him back to England, the first South Sea Islander to visit that country.

The team saw similarities between Cook's ship and the new orbiter. The earlier ship was equipped, like the orbiter, with the newest equipment of its time; the orbiter uses the newest technology in navigation as did *Adventure*. Each flight of the orbiter improves upon and learns from the last, as Cook's expeditions did. The first *Adventure* circumnavigated Earth on the sea, and the orbiter circles Earth in space. The first *Adventure* was looking for new knowledge about Earth and its unknown regions, as the orbiter does in space.

The team concluded with, "America was built upon the spirit of adventure. It took tremendous courage and foresight for those earlier explorers to venture forth and challenge the unknown, as America's space program does today. We look to space as a place of growth, mystery, and new experiences. It is something that excites and stimulates the imagination of everyone."

Life Aboard a Sea Vessel vs. an Orbiter

In their project, which they divided into two phases, the team simulated and compared the experiences of living and working aboard a sea vessel from the 1770s and the orbiter of the 1980s.

Phase I. Sea Vessel Experience

In Phase I, the team focused on community resources. They discovered a program that offered a unique experience: to become overnight crew members aboard a sea vessel from about *Adventure's* time, living and working as crews did 200 years ago. They researched conditions on *Adventure* and prepared a list of questions to ask the captain and crew. They also asked to be provided with information and a hands-on experience with the navigational equipment available in the 1770s. They invited the rest of the class to participate, and everyone was assigned tasks to undertake while aboard ship.

Phase II. Orbiter Experience

They returned to the library to conduct more research and to the community to visit two aerospace industries: first, McDonnell Douglas to view a mock-up of the Space Station the United States plans to build and to learn what part the orbiter will play in its construction and use; then to Rockwell International to see a full-scale wooden mock-up of an orbiter. With their newly acquired knowledge and "imaginations on overdrive," they called upon parents and community for help. At a general meeting, they explained their idea of building a mock-up of an orbiter suitable for a simulated flight.

The team divided this part of the project into the construction phase and the simulated flight phase. Taking each one a step at a time, they listed what would be entailed in the construction phase, and from the list and the talents and interests of the people involved, they created an exterior design team, an interior design team, a construction team, a materials acquisition team, and an art team. The guidelines: The mock-up would be one-half size; it would be built in stages, which would have to be light and ready for final assembly the day before the simulated launch; the cargo bay would serve as a sleeping area; there would be no wheels; and materials would have to be inexpensive. They set a launch date and worked backwards to set up deadlines for each phase of the construction. They visited businesses in the community to explain their project and needs. Three construction companies donated materials as did many parents.

Ideas for the simulated flight: Flight plan of 14 orbits for the 14 team members; the time required, and then the launch and landing times; a circular orbit that would cross the route of Cook's *Adventure;* and a computer program, "Time and Miles in Space," that would let them know exactly where they were at any given moment.

Scientific experiments to be conducted: In botany, "Do plant roots grow down in a weightless condition?" and "What direction will the roots grow in zero 'G' when they hit the wall of a flower pot?"; in biology, the effects microgravity would have on a snake shedding its skin; in chemistry, growing basic crystals. It was decided that control experiments would be conducted by students not making the simulated flight. They also asked other classes to provide small self-contained payloads for the mission.

Other activities: Each team member selected an area to be flown over for which he or she would prepare and present a five-minute geography lesson; they took a computer programmed with flight simulation exercises, and a VCR and television set to play two tapes during recreation periods; and each team member would keep a personal journal.

As a living tribute to the *Challenger* astronauts from the schoolchildren of America, they took along a package of their state's flower seeds. They were symbolic of an idea they plan to submit to NASA for consideration: to take seeds of each State's flower on a future Shuttle mission and then plant them at or near Mission Control in Houston in memory of the *Challenger* crew.

Realism was added with tapes of an actual liftoff and landing. They designed a lighting system for the orbiter and added some screen magic to the computer program to add the effect of day and night; a hospital donated uniforms and the team designed a personal mission patch and acquired space food. Extravehicular activities were conducted to go to the restroom. A local fire department donated extinguishers to simulate the special effects of the launch, and the police department took aerial photographs and provided surveillance.

Postmission activities included developing lesson plans around NASA spinoffs, careers, and additional scientific investigations.

Model for the Future

The project has potential as a model for future classroom and school activities. It can be used as a theme for integrating the academic disciplines. It can also serve as a model for students, faculty, and parents working together toward a common goal. The process employed in the project of research, documentation, and activities can be incorporated into classroom and school activities, regardless of theme. The project also demonstrates that learning is an exciting and rewarding adventure.

Endeavour

Moorish idol, species of butterfly fish found in coral reefs, *zoological drawing made by Sydney Parkinson on Cook's first voyage. Courtesy of The Natural History Museum, London.*

Why *Endeavour*

We chose our name *Endeavour* after the 1760's sailing ship, a North Sea bark. It, like the *Challenger*, was refitted and improved upon. It was a sturdy and reliable ship that was equipped with great care to take its crew around the world.

There are several reasons we feel the *Endeavour* would be the best name:

ABNER BAKER
ELEMENTARY SCHOOL
300 Lake Street
Fort Morgan, Colorado 80701

Joan K. Zack
Team Coordinator
Coordinator, Gifted and
Talented Programs, K-5

TEAM MEMBERS
GRADE 3

Sylvia Barros
Mark Edson
James Greenwood
Doug Jones
Quentin Mese
Mike Molesworth
Jay Musgrave
Chris Piatz

1 The ship carried scientists and the most innovative equipment on its journey. Marine surveyors, astronomers, botanists, zoologists, artists, mathematicians, and a physician were all a part of the crew. Best known of this scientific crew were Captain Cook, Joseph Banks (botanist and zoologist), and Daniel Solander (Swedish botanist). The ship also carried such innovative equipment as the Harrison chronometer, a precision timepiece which won the British Parliament's award for accuracy in determining latitude and longitude.

2 The ship and its crew were the first ship to accurately and system-atically explore and chart much of the South Pacific. The ship spent six months circumnavigating and mapping the 2,400 mile coastline of New Zealand and proved that it was not attached to a mythical southern continent, Terra Australis. The ship then mapped the eastern coast of Australia.

3 Its captain was outstanding in his endeavours. He volunteered to be a Royal Navy seaman even though he could have had an easier life and better pay in private trade. We feel Captain Cook displayed courage and patriotism in his choices. He was precise in his calculations and journals. He was trusted and respected. These are traits that we feel are important to us and our space program.

4 Preservation of life and health were valued by the captain and crew. The *Endeavour* was one of the first ships to prevent scurvy on board such a long journey. Their careful records of the steps they took to prevent scurvy allowed the entire British fleet to virtually eliminate scurvy by 1800.

5 Even in that early day, the *Endeavour's* primary purpose was related to space exploration; it was to observe the transit of the planet Venus from Tahiti.

6 The word endeavour means to strive for . . . to make an effort. That is what each of us must do to succeed; each of us in school, at work, on land, and in space must endeavour to do his or her best.

An Orbiter for Teaching Materials

The entire third grade was immersed in the study of space and flight during the fall semester, 1988. The project team members were selected for above-average ability, achievement, creativity, and task commitment. Research, planning, and development of the model were done jointly by the team and adult volunteers with donated materials.

The model orbiter is over nine feet tall, rolls on casters, and has a removable nose section to allow it to travel into classrooms. It is used to house NASA teaching materials and additional materials related to flight and space in almost all school-related subjects.

The size of the model is very appealing to the primary age students at Abner Baker, a school for grades K-3. It creates an initial student interest in space and allows the teacher to borrow and to contribute materials directly related to space and flight.

Two related "endeavours" were developed by the art and music teachers: a theme song, which was recorded by the third-grade classes and placed in the orbiter; and a design contest for a logo for the third-grade students, with the winning entry made into a button for the team. The artist was invited to join the team.

Model for the Future

The orbiter can be duplicated easily by any school. It will be of use for many years, because it houses projects that allow teachers to teach a thematic unit, drawing together all academic subjects from materials supplied through NASA, created locally, and purchased from publishers. Many can be used by older students to teach younger children. In addition, teachers are encouraged to submit one new learning guide for each week that they check out the orbiter, keeping supplies growing and current. A master copy of each learning unit is kept on file outside the orbiter to prevent loss.

All portions of this
section are perma-
nently attached. This
section is removable
& houses a shelf
(bottom of upper
barrel) which is
used for a tape
recorder, VCR or
movie projector.

bottom of
inverted barrel

large detergent
barrels

disk of ½" plywood
for shelf. Notches
cut out for 1x4
supports.

Grooves in barrel
allow shelf to be
held & supported.

electrical
tape used
for
markings

disk of 1"
plywood with 4
casters inserted
through holes.

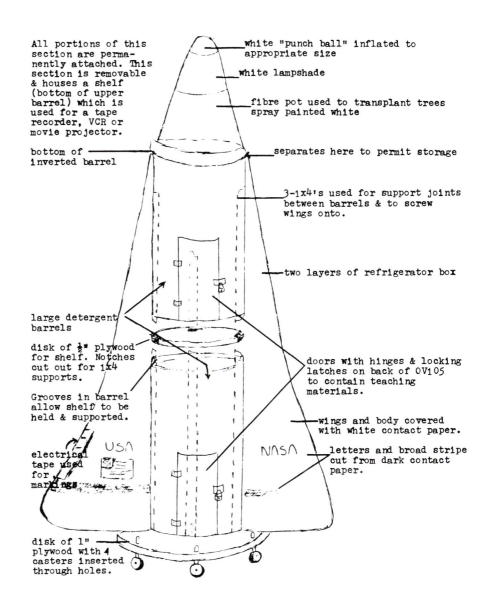

white "punch ball" inflated to
appropriate size

white lampshade

fibre pot used to transplant trees
spray painted white

separates here to permit storage

3-1x4's used for support joints
between barrels & to screw
wings onto.

two layers of refrigerator box

doors with hinges & locking
latches on back of OV105
to contain teaching
materials.

wings and body covered
with white contact paper.

letters and broad stripe
cut from dark contact
paper.

USA

NASA

Endeavour

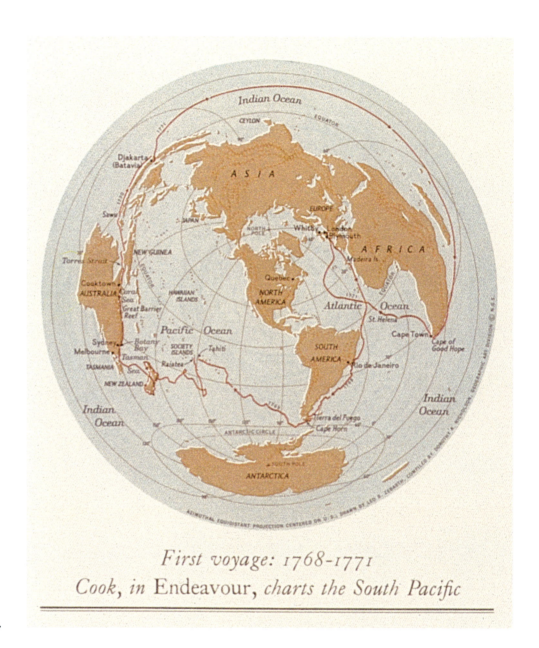

First voyage: 1768-1771
Cook, in Endeavour, charts the South Pacific

*Map of Cook's first voyage.
(c) National Geographic
Society. Used with permission.*

Why *Endeavour*

A.H. ROCKWELL
ELEMENTARY SCHOOL
Whittlesey Drive
Bethel, Connecticut 06801

Rosemary I. Payne
Team Coordinator
Teacher and Unit Coordinator
Grades Pre-1-3
Language arts,
math, and science

TEAM MEMBERS, PRE-1-6

Heather Babington (3)
Ryan Burke (4)
Pat Chieffalo (6)
Jeffrey Cullen (3)
Conor Evans (3)
Dana Griffin (2)
Erin Hammond (5)
Ryan Hill (2)
Steven Hubbard (3)
Teddy Kelsey (6)
Brett Lefferts (4)
Eli Lefferts (2)
Devon McGuinness (5)
Shelby McLoughlin (6)
Will Michaels (Pre-1)
Jenny Nolan (5)
Elizabeth Noyce (3)
Anthony Pasciucco (2)
Leah Rafalko (4)
Jennifer Reynolds (6)
Keegan Shaw (6)
Michele Struna (5)
Allyson Trowbridge (4)
Ryan Trowbridge (K)
Melissa Tucci (4)

The *Endeavour* was a sea vessel selected for a unique expedition in 1768. It was the first British ship ever directed towards scientific discovery. The *Endeavour* was selected because it was a sturdy ship which would be traveling to the recently discovered island of Tahiti in the uncertain waters of the Pacific Ocean. The purpose of the exploration was to study the passage of Venus across the sun. This observation would determine the distance of the sun from the Earth. Naturalists on board the *Endeavour* collected samples of local plants and animals. Sketches of samples, islanders, and landscape were captured in drawings, which helped to create the beautiful image of the South Seas island.

The British Admirality, however, had a secret mission in mind for Captain James Cook. After completing astronomical observations, he was to look for an unknown continent south of Tahiti, chart its coast, and claim it for England. Cook accomplished this mission successfully by sighting the southeast corner of Australia. He sailed farther and explored more of the South Sea than anyone had done before. He traveled 2,500 miles in less than six months on an unfamiliar and very dangerous coast.

The Rockwell School Space Shuttle Team (RSSST) feels that the next Space Shuttle would appropriately be named after this sturdy sea-vessel, because this voyage was the first British ship involved in a mission involving the study of space. Both the announced goals and the secret instructions were accomplished, ... The *Endeavour's* voyage was so worthwhile that Cook was given permission and support to lead more investigations. Continued space exploration is crucial and we trust that with future discoveries and successes, this will reinforce the spirit and support of America's mission in space.

On July 26, 1971, the Apollo 15 was launched to explore the Hadley-Rille Apennine area of the moon . . . . This was the fourth manned lunar landing mission and one of the greatest and most ambitious space explorations of the lunar surface. For the first time, the astronauts conducted a motorized exploration of the moon's surface. For the first time, a lunar navigation device was used. For the first time, the first subsatellite was launched into lunar orbit. . . .

We must continue our endeavors to face the challenge of outer space with great drive and determination. And so the Rockwell School Space Shuttle Team endorses the name *Endeavour* as the name of our next space shuttle. It is our hope that this name will remind us all of man's past limitless abilities and successes in space exploration and will encourage optimism towards present and future space missions. Only then may we keep the dream of the *Challenger* crew alive.

ENDEAVOR TO MEET THE CHALLENGE!

The Rockwell Shuttle Program

Rockwell School teachers were asked by the team coordinator to send two volunteers from their classrooms, grades 2-6, and one student to represent kindergarten and grade 1, who would be interested in working on a school research team to select a name for the new NASA orbiter, OV-105.

At the initial meeting, students were told that all meetings' contents and eventual chosen name would be a secret and were not to be shared with fellow classmates until presented to the entire school in January 1989. This added an air of excitement and importance to their mission.

Four groups of the RSSST Committee researched various names of seaworthy vessels, supported their suggestions with rationales, and in turn presented them to their team members. Each of the four teams voted for the one they felt was the best choice from among *Dolphin, Goodspeed,* and *Endeavour,* which was proposed by two teams. After a final committee vote, *Endeavour* won. The RSSST felt that naming the new orbiter *Endeavour* would encourage all Americans to continually strive for and seek out excellence and work for success, no matter what hardship one might face. The name *Endeavour* also sends a very special message to America's students—that they must always endeavor to be the best that they can be!

The Rockwell team included five adult leaders, three teachers, and two parent/community members. Additional support was received from the school's media specialist and physical education instructor. Many of the team members' parents supported their children with help in the preparation of Shuttle research and activities, all designed to enrich the school's curriculum areas and to reinforce learning in the classrooms. Additional research materials were gathered by the Bethel, Danbury, and Western Connecticut State College librarians, who were most supportive in the team's search and research for appropriate materials. The 25 student-team members were divided into four groups, each with a leader(s).

First voyage: 1768-1771
Cook, in Endeavour, charts the South Pacific

- GROUP I, under the direction of the music instructor and a musician-parent, wrote a theme song after *Endeavour* was selected. The students, using their learned skills of poetry and music structuring, told a story in words and music about the Shuttle. With cooperation and guidance, the completed music arrangement and lyrics were presented to the entire committee for approval. Two meetings were spent rehearsing the song. At the last session, the physical education instructor presented an exercise routine to *Endeavour's* theme-song music, which had been worked out with students.

- GROUP II, headed by a parent, worked mainly on researching the history of *Endeavour* and the Apollo 15 mission. They recognized a strong correlation between the two explorations and wanted this to be recognized and valued in the team's choice of the name *Endeavour.* The team also coordinated map study skills; they plotted *Endeavour's* route and discoveries and completed a large clay map depicting James Cook's explorations.

First voyage: 1768-1771
Cook, in Endeavour, charts the South Pacific

■ GROUP III, under the direction of the third grade teacher, undertook the creation of games and activities that would enhance all curriculum areas. The activities were designed to be expanded and adapted by staff and students for all grade levels and to be used in student learning centers or in small and large group presentations, K-6. Each classroom was to receive a complete packet of all space-related activities and games.

■ GROUP IV worked with the team coordinator to accomplish several tasks. Two team members, with help from their family, created a colorful board game called Shuttle Launch Trivia. It was developed with Shuttle playing-pieces and science-related trivia questions. A local printer reproduced copies of the game board for all Rockwell School classrooms. Another team member designed a Shuttle logo.

On January 12, 1989, the RSSST's, in specially designed silk-screened tee shirts, planned to present to the Rockwell School student body, parents, invited guests, community members, and media reporters a Rockwell Shuttle Program to share their weeks of effort.

Model for the Future

RSSST's multidisciplinary learning activities packet is intended to stimulate teacher and student creativity, knowledge, and expertise in all subjects. The teacher may adapt the activities to his or her grade level.

Phoenix

Phoenix *by Charles B.*
Lawrence. Courtesy of The
Mariners' Museum, Newport
News, Virginia.

Why *Phoenix*

RICHARDSON PARK
LEARNING CENTER
99 Middleboro Road
Wilmington, Delaware 19804

Cynthia L. Pochomis
Team Coordinator
Special Education Teacher
Grades 3-6

TEAM MEMBERS
GRADES 4-6

Keith Evans (5)
Jeff Hensley (4)
Jesse Hughart (6)
Christine Jones (4)
Crystal McDowell (4)
Graphton Peterson (5)
Eve Pia (4)
Jamie Powers (5)
Mary Riccio (5)
Deshawn Scott (5)
Lashonda Selby (5)
Kelly Taylor (5)
Kevin Timm (6)

The name our class has chosen for the spacecraft is the *Phoenix.* There are many ways that this name is perfect for the new OV 105.

The steamship *Phoenix* was invented by Robert Stevens. It was a very successful commercial ship which helped to make steamships an important means of navigation in the 1800's. It was part of a group of experimental steamships being developed by Robert Fulton, William Symington, and John Stevens. It was the first steamboat to navigate the open seas. Just like the *Phoenix,* the new space shuttle will have many "firsts" and will be an important means of space navigation in the 2000's.

In mythology, the Phoenix was a bird that could bring itself back to life after it was destroyed by fire. It was a rare and beautiful bird that lived in the Temple of the Sun in Egypt. This school year the theme for our class has been the Phoenix. Our teacher tells us that just like the bird we will all try to rise above the disabilities we have and become the best people we can be. Instead of looking at our weaknesses, we focus on our strengths and work hard at improving them.

The new space shuttle will have to be a rare and beautiful bird that will have to rise above the terrible tragedy of the Challenger explosion. But just like the Phoenix myth, it will come back stronger and better than ever, ready to carry on America's mission in space.

All American school children are proud of our space shuttle and through television, we feel as though we are a part of each flight. We are very happy to have been included in this contest.

A Project in "Living Skills"

At the beginning of each school year, the students' teacher chooses a theme for the class to use as a cohesive element throughout the year. The 1988-89 theme was the phoenix. The students heard the story of the phoenix and were told how, just like the mythical bird, they could rise above their problems. "She always tells us that we are the best class in the school and that we are special people."

This project was designed to provide practice in living skills that will benefit the students throughout their lifetimes. When the team discussed names that would be good for a Shuttle, they liked bird names, especially eagle and condor, but their favorite name was phoenix. Excited about the orbiter-naming competition, when they learned the name had to be that of a ship, they worried they wouldn't find a *Phoenix.* But first, they had to decide all the things they would need to learn to do a research project to find a ship named *Phoenix.* They chose good telephone manners, reading a bus schedule, library skills, and a computer search.

- They invited a computer-information expert from the Delaware Teacher Center to class to learn about their project and to run a computer search for them. They were very happy to learn they could use their name. Not only was there a *Phoenix,* but it sailed up the Delaware River to Philadelphia not far from their school.

- Next, they began lessons in telephoning and schedule reading. Using play telephones, they role-played several situations. After sufficient practice, they called the library and bus station to obtain information on fares, schedules, hours, and to make an appointment at the public library to do research.

- They learned to read a bus schedule and traveled by public transportation from school to town to do their research. To pay for the trip, they made vegetable soup and sold it to the faculty.

- At the library they were given a tour and taught a lesson in card cataloguing. They learned more about the phoenix and saw pictures of how it looked to different artists. The librarian also helped them look up their steamship. Then the students extended their research to see if other ships were named after other mythological creatures.

- Each student researched a ship or character and wrote down some facts for a final report. Back in school, they dictated stories to the team coordinator and put them together in book form; then one of the students made some sketches to illustrate it.

Model for the Future

"This project enabled the children to view themselves as capable individuals who could complete a project from start to finish and compete on a national level. . . . the boost in self-esteem was the main reason for entering the contest and that goal was certainly accomplished.

"A project of this type lends itself to every area of the curriculum. Lessons were conducted in reading, speaking, math, writing, living skills and social studies. The children became 'turned on' by the project itself and are now more enthusiastic about doing research. Because they realize that they are capable, they know that any topic they wish to explore is now open to them."

In 1856 the clipper Neptune's Car arrived in San Francisco. The commander was the captain's wife Mary Patten. She had been in charge for 52 days dealing successfully with navigating around the Horn with discipline problems and a dying husband. She was only 19 years old and 4 months pregnant.

Kelly Taylor

THETIS

The Thetis was a sailing ship in which Richard Wagner crossed the Baltic Sea. When a storm came up Wagner remembered the legend of the Flying Dutchman. He was inspired to write his first famous opera The Flying Dutchman.

Lashonda Selby

From The *Phoenix* and other Ships Named for Mythological Creatures. *Illustrations by Jesse Hughart.*

THE PHOENIX

An American made steamship, The Phoenix was launched in 1807. It was the first steamship to sail in the ocean. It sailed up the Delaware River to Philadelphia. It was built by John Stevens and his son Robert.

Mary Riccio

25

Resolution

Portrait of Captain James Cook *by John Webber, 1776. (c) National Art Gallery, Wellington, New Zealand. Used with permission.*

Why *Resolution*

PEARL RIDGE
ELEMENTARY SCHOOL
98-940 Moanalua Road
Aiea, Hawaii 96701

Marie Ann Kohara
Team Coordinator
Teacher, Grades 5-6

TEAM MEMBERS
GRADE 6

Sean Arakawa
Gina Gormley
Justin Greges
Tara McRae
Shandis Moy
Marti Townsend
Adriane Uganiza
William Francis Woo
Roger Yamane
Darin Yap

We strongly believe that the name *Resolution*, Captain James Cook's exploration vessel and the sister ship of *Discovery*, should be given to OV-105. The name *Resolution* which is easy to pronounce for radio transmission is appropriate for OV-105 because it sounds like it has goals to achieve. It captures the spirit of America's mission in space with its definition . . . a promise.

In selecting the name *Resolution*, we considered how the missions and accomplishments of Captain Cook's *Resolution* were related to those of America's space program. Cook's mission on the *Resolution* during his voyage II was to search for a great southern continent. On January 17, 1773, the *Resolution* was the first ship to ever cross the Antarctic Circle. During this voyage, Cook was the first to observe the Aurora Australis. When Cook was 75 miles from the Antarctic continent, large ice fields forced him to turn back. Although Cook failed to find the great southern continent, he did believe that there might be land past the ice because he saw sea birds. That land he felt would be inhospitable. Just as the *Resolution* searched for new lands and surveyed little known ones, our astronauts seek new information as they survey the solar system. Perhaps a new planet will be discovered, one that will be suitable for human life.

Cook took a crew of trained specialists as well as sailors on this second voyage. John Forster and his son, John George Adam, were two German naturalists who sailed with Cook. So did astronomer William Wales who was to do position-fixing using lunars and to test marine chronometers. They wanted to find out if the chronometer would provide an easier and more accurate method of calculating longitude. Cook's respect for the instrument helped it to perform successfully, a very important result of this voyage. Cook and his crew used their instruments skillfully giving us a very complete charting of the Pacific. Like a scientist, Cook surveyed and mapped the coastlines several times to make sure that the measurements were accurate. As on the *Resolution*, the space shuttle crew is made up of specialists: the commander, pilot, payload specialist, and mission specialists. Each is highly trained to perform specific duties and to use their instruments skillfully. . . .

During his voyage III on the *Resolution*, Captain Cook unsuccessfully searched for a northwest passage to the Atlantic. However, he did prove that ice made a northwest route impracticable. He also discovered in January 1778 five islands (Oahu, Kauai, Niihau, and the islets of Lehua and Kaula) which he called the Sandwich Islands. There he made friends with the natives and was given fresh provisions. Through his detailed notes, we learned much about the government, religion, costumes, culture, and customs of the natives. Cook regarded this discovery of the Sandwich Islands (later called Hawaiian Islands) as his most important discovery

because of their central location in the vast Pacific Ocean. It was a place to rest, to get provisions and fresh water, and to make any needed repairs. He could see then what the islands would mean to ships of the future. Like the Sandwich Islands, the space station of the 1990s will be a port of call for the space shuttle. It will provide a place to dock, to get new supplies, or to be repaired. The space station is the future of our space shuttle program.

In 1991, the OV-105 will make her maiden voyage for the United States of America. She will be delivering a promise that began during the presidency of John F. Kennedy when he proclaimed that the United States would not retreat from the challenges of space. When OV-105 sails through the vast ocean in the sky, may she proudly wear the name *Resolution,* a symbol of our country's promise and determination to reach for the stars.

Nil intentatum reliquit (Nothing left untried): Cook's motto on his coat of arms

Hawaii and the Space Station

The team wanted to do a play. Brainstorming brought a plan to have Captain Cook meet some astronauts and share experiences of his that are related to space missions. But because Captain Cook is no longer living, the students had a problem! Then someone remembered a storybook that they had read called *A Wrinkle in Time.* In it, the characters could travel through space and time by "tessering." The team liked the idea and agreed to have Captain Cook "tesser" through time and space. Then they decided to use characters from the book and write their play as a sequel. The theme would be Captain Cook's motto, "Nothing left untried," combined with the idea that the U.S. Space Shuttle is a resolution, a promise to continue the space program with renewed confidence.

Once they selected their project, the team divided the tasks: scriptwriting and constructing the Space Station.

■ Those who wrote the script worked individually at times. Then they met in an "elbow group" (a support group that listens to someone's writing and offers criticism). They then combined ideas they liked into one script. At other times they collaborated orally and wrote the script together. The entire team, serving as an elbow group when the script was finished, helped by pointing out relationships between Cook's voyage and the Space Shuttle's mission that were missing from the script.

■ The Space Station fit in perfectly with the play because it could be used in one of the scenes with the commander of the Shuttle and Cook. To help explain the model, the students felt they needed a diagram showing the cross section of the Space Station and descriptions of its various facilities.

■ They reviewed everyone's designs and combined them into a sketch for the model and selected a scale to use. Materials were discussed and cardboard decided for use, but building the Space Station was more difficult than expected. Cutting the cardboard was a problem and took too long, so they decided to use Lego tiles, which were easier, faster, and safer.

■ The facilities: The *laboratory* is divided into two floors, chemistry and biomedical; on the lower biomedical floor, tests, surveys, and experiments are conducted on plants, small animals, and the astronauts to find out the effects of living in microgravity. A central processing unit in the laboratory receives or sends information to Earth. An *observatory* contains a giant telescope. The *assembly room* is where new parts for the Shuttle and satellites are made; most work is done by a remote manipulator arm that is controlled by a manned computer linked to the main computer for receiving commands and processing data. *Living facilities* include the kitchen, which is equipped with a device for rehydrating food and a washer that cleans utensils with a disinfecting spray; sleeping quarters for each astronaut; and a small gym for keeping astronauts in condition. There is a storage room under the laboratory for equipment and spare parts; the goods are kept in boxes and moved by a remote-controlled crane.

While the model was being built, some students sketched the cross section; others wrote descriptions of the facilities. They used a second scale to make a large drawing of the model, then a copier to enlarge it even more. They colored the drawings, cut them out, and glued them on black paper sprinkled with glitter to make it look like an outer-space scene.

Model for the Future

This project can be adapted for use with grades K-12. In the primary grades, the research can be simplified with oral reading of the material by the teacher and notetaking done together on a chart. From the notes, a collaborative essay can be written. Then an informal skit can be created by role-playing the parts of the explorer and the astronauts. The children can do free-writing and journal or log-writing. Their ideas can be combined into a story or a poem and published. Using large building blocks, a Space Station can be built to their design. For the secondary level, the project can be carried out at a level of greater difficulty and using relevant content.

Victoria

FERDINAND MAGELLAN.

(From a Portrait in the Versailles Collection.)

Frontispiece from The Life of Ferdinand Magellan *by Dr. F. H. H. Guillemard. London: George Philip & Son, 1890. Courtesy of Library of Congress.*

30

Why *Victoria*

CHENOWETH
ELEMENTARY SCHOOL
3600 Brownsboro Road
Louisville, Kentucky 40207

Cindy A. Ellis
Team Coordinator
Kindergarten Teacher

TEAM MEMBERS

48 kindergarten students
14 fifth-grade students

The Chenoweth team chose *Victoria* in honor of Ferdinand Magellan, leader of the first ocean expedition to circumnavigate the globe. With five ships and about 270 men of many nationalities, he sailed across the Atlantic to South America. Before reaching the passage now known as the Strait of Magellan, one ship was wrecked and its crew joined the other vessels. On October 21, 1520, the ships entered the strait. During their travel through the passage, another ship deserted the expedition and returned to Spain. On November 28, the remaining three vessels reached the body of water Magellan named the Pacific Ocean.

The following spring, Magellan's expedition reached Guam, and sailed on to the islands later named the Philippines. There, the great navigator and explorer became involved in a local war and was killed on April 27, 1521. Only one ship, *Victoria,* survived the rigorous voyage back to Spain, arriving in September 1522. Although he did not complete the journey, Magellan's skill and determination made the first circumnavigation possible.

The Chenoweth team believed Magellan's ship *Victoria* is an appropriate name for a spacecraft for several reasons:

- The name elicits the feeling of victory, a conquest over the unknown or unexplained;

- Victoria has been used for the name of a medal awarded for acts of valor;

- Organizations, such as the American Legion and Knights of Columbus, have used it for honor awards;

- It is unique to American history as the name of an open-passenger automobile with a folding top, thus the first convertible, passion of America since the building of Henry Ford's mechanical moving machines.

Victoria as a spacecraft would represent challenge, valor, honor, and innovativeness and capture the spirit of America's mission in space through its pioneer spirit. Also, *Victoria* would be the first ship of its type to bear a female's name.

A Project for Two Grades

As part of the regular Chenoweth Elementary School program, fifth-graders tutor kindergarten children working under the direction of the kindergarten teacher in the kindergarten setting. This relationship continued with the orbiter-naming project. After the fifth-graders did the basic research on sea vessels, they took their reports with visuals to present to the kindergarten students. At this point, a list of vessels' names was developed for consideration.

The team project began when the children voted to build a replica of the orbiter, which they had named *Victoria*. The two groups designed and built the orbiter together, a six-foot base structure made of cardboard covered with papier-mâché and painted with identifying markings (windows, name, etc.).

FERDINAND MAGELLAN.
(From a Portrait in the Versailles Collection.)

Learning Goals—Fifth Grade
Research

- Gain knowledge of sea and land explorers

- Gain knowledge of conditions of the times (hardships, tools, equipment, and technological advancements)

- Research, writing, and report-organization skills

- Decision-making processes

- Reading books for pleasure

- Use of computers for research

Model Building

- Creating and following design

- Use of cardboard construction, papier-mâché, and paint

- Creative display of finished product

Interaction

- Tutoring

- Individual work reports

- Small group model project

- Large group report-sharing with kindergarten children

Learning Goals—Kindergarten
Beginning awareness of space

- Follow-up of watching *Discovery* launch

- Working with the direction of tutors in developing Shuttle design

Language Experience

- Awareness of space terminology introduced in individual projects and the book *Cat In Space*

- Illustrating *Cat in Space*

- Imaginative stories about a trip into space, what an alien might look like, telling a story of what life might be like on another planet

Mathematics

- Count, measure, compare, approximate, and use geometrical design

- Coordination of mathematical grade-learning levels and exchanging of mathematical skills

FERDINAND MAGELLAN.
(From a Portrait in the Versailles Collection.)

There were special activities for both groups: a field trip to a planetarium and the National History Museum's Star Lab, stories about space, and weekly instruction in library skills. The kindergarteners used their home libraries as well as community resources, such as the Natural History Museum's space exhibit, where they delighted in hands-on experiences: sitting in a Gemini capsule, space food, space suits, seeing a computer like the one NASA uses to track the orbiter.

Of the 48 kindergarten children involved with their families in the project, 45 completed a take-home space project—a fantastic percentage.

Model for the Future

As a model for future classroom and school activities, the potential for this project is limited only by the imagination and excitement of the teachers and students.

Dove

Maryland Dove. *Photo by Jack Hevey. Courtesy of Historic St. Mary's City, Maryland.*

Why *Dove*

HOMESTEAD-WAKEFIELD
ELEMENTARY SCHOOL
900 South Main Street
Bel Air, Maryland 21014

Elizabeth M. Burley
Team Coordinator
Teacher, Grade 4

TEAM MEMBERS

Emily Borneman
Dorothy Brooke
Shelly Duguid
Tim Gaeng
Christina Garvine
Greg Henneman
Jessica Huckeba
Sarah Ann Ill
Chen Liang
Matt Linz
Brenda Mikanowicz
Matt Mikos
Stacey O'Connor
Lee Park
Farah Patel
Bobby Pohlner
Joe Popp
Ryan Pouncy
Saud Rahman
Pat Ruese
Richard Schwartz
Alex Siegel
Micah Sobus
Shikha Srivastava
Emily Stevenson
Chris Stewart
Kelly Storck
Scott Stronski
Brad Walker
Jennifer Ward

In choosing a name for Space Shuttle Orbiter Vehicle 105, we looked back into our home state's history. Our choice of *Dove* as our entry is related to the settlement of the Maryland colony as well as the symbolic nature of the bird itself which, we feel, captures the spirit of America's mission in space.

The colony of Maryland began when George Calvert, the first Lord Baltimore, petitioned Charles I of England for a site for a colony. At this time everyone was being forced to attend the same church as the king. Lord Baltimore wanted to establish a colony where all people were free to worship as they pleased. He was granted a site in Newfoundland called Avalon, which turned out to be a failure.

Upon George Calvert's death, his son, Cecil, became the second Lord Baltimore and carried out his father's wish for freedom by seeking and being granted an area farther south which became known as Maryland. To settle the new colony, Lord Baltimore engaged two vessels, the *Ark* and the *Dove,* to carry people and supplies to the New World in the name of freedom.

The *Dove* was a two masted pinnace and very small when compared to the *Ark.* It acted as the supply ship for the settlers who were carried on the *Ark.* The supplies for the voyage were well planned by Lord Baltimore since he did not want the Maryland colony to fail for the reasons Avalon did - sickness and starvation. He planned food supplies to last a year, tools and equipment for building houses, and seed for crops. All this relates very well to the mission of the shuttle in the possible establishment of a space station and future colonization in space because the shuttle will be the supply ship for this kind of development.

During the voyage to the New World, the tiny *Dove* was forced to turn back to England because of a violent storm. However, once the storm had passed, it set out alone and completed the journey, rejoining the *Ark* in Barbados. In doing this, the crew of the *Dove* displayed a strong determination to succeed, a great deal of courage, and a belief in themselves and the importance of their mission. These are all characteristics that we feel are shared by the astronauts who are involved in America's space program.

We also chose the name *Dove* because of the symbolic nature of the bird itself. The dove is a symbol of exploration. A dove was sent out from the Ark by Noah to search for land following the great flood. In this same way, America's space program sends the shuttle in search of new frontiers. The dove is a messenger of peace and freedom. As our space program probes deeper and deeper into the frontier of space, it will bring the message of peace and freedom to our world and the worlds beyond ours.

A Language Arts Project

The team felt their name choice was a good one because it would lead to researching their state's history and because the *Dove* was named after a symbol of peace. They wanted to link the *Dove's* voyage to Maryland with a Shuttle's voyage into space.

They began their project by collecting references dealing with the state's history and NASA's Shuttle program, using resources at school, books from the county library, and material from Historic St. Mary's City, site of the Maryland settlement. A parent brought a prize-winning dove to class to introduce the dove's feeding habits, how it raises its young, and where they come from. She also told the class many funny stories about having a dove in the house.

Because they were a large language arts class, the team decided to divide the class into three small groups and to choose three small projects.

The Voyage to Maryland and *3-2-1 Blast Off!*

One of the small groups developed story books for primary age children, which told about the voyage to Maryland and the Shuttle program in words that a young child could understand. The group decided to write two short books instead of one long one because, writing for young children, they knew shorter was better for short attention spans. They titled their books *The Voyage to Maryland* and *3-2-1 Blast Off!* and placed them in the school library.

Dream to the Future

The second group wrote a play that could be produced for the school's annual Maryland Day celebration. They linked *Dove's* voyage to Maryland and a Shuttle voyage with a dream sequence. Once the acts were sketched out, the group was directed to add more facts about the space program—living in space, past and present astronauts, etc. The resulting play, *Dream to the Future,* was planned for production in March 1989 by the entire class.

Ship and Shuttle Trivia

The third group linked *Dove's* voyage and the Shuttle program by creating a game for the school library for use by the intermediate students. Called Ship and Shuttle Trivia, the group put together 72 questions and answers dealing with Maryland's early history and the space program. They designed a circular game board similar to a Trivial Pursuit board, and used the school's computers to produce their questions on cards which were then laminated.

Model for the Future

As a model for future activities, the team felt that they produced items that could be used in many different ways. Their story books were good literature to enjoy, but also could be used as models for future writers. The play, on the other hand, provides an audience with both entertainment and knowledge of facts; it also increases its participants' public speaking skills.

The game was created as an example of learning as fun. The students felt that it could be used as a follow-up to curriculum-related lessons or as a review before a test. They also felt that their questions were difficult enough to motivate the players to find the answers, thereby enhancing their learning.

The team and their coordinator planned to share all the projects with the people who helped them. When the staff from Historic St. Mary's City requested copies of their efforts, they began to pursue ways to produce their work for public enjoyment.

Adventure

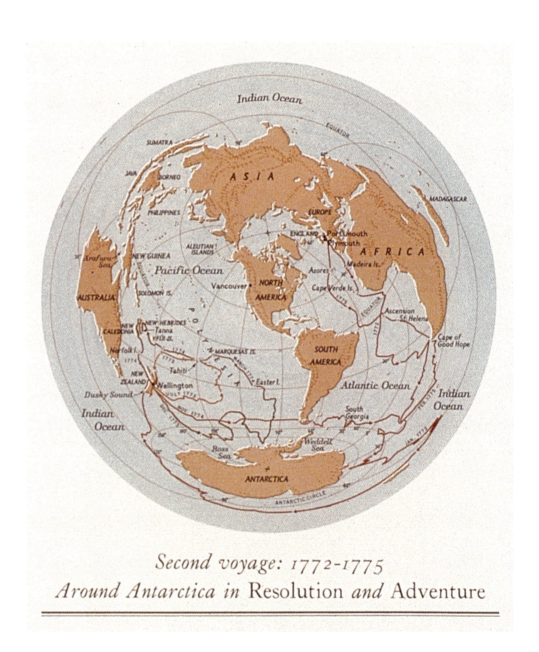

Second voyage: 1772-1775
Around Antarctica in Resolution *and* Adventure

Map of Cook's second voyage. (c) National Geographic Society. Used with permission.

Why *Adventure*

CLINTON COUNTY R-III
ELLIS ELEMENTARY

603 Frost
Plattsburg, Missouri 64477

Rose Diane Warren
Team Coordinator
Teacher, Grade 4

TEAM MEMBERS
44 fourth-grade students

Adventure was the name of an exploring, sea vessel. The main captain of the ship was James Cook. Captain Furneaux took command of the ship also. Along with the ship called *Resolution*, *Adventure* sailed south from England to search for a southern continent.

The journey began in the middle of July in 1772, and took three years to complete the trip. Captain Cook and the crews' mission was to find out how far north the ice went from the southern continent which we call Antarctica today. In 1773, they crossed what is now called the Antarctic Circle. The *Adventure* and the *Resolution* were the first ships to cross into this far southern region. They kept sailing south for a short time, but the packed ice ahead of them made them turn back north and then east. Captain Cook sailed around Antarctica without seeing land. Captain Cook wasn't aware that he had come within 150 miles of the Antarctic shore. From this exploration, Cook found out that because of the icy seas and the risks involved in exploring the Antarctic, no one would ever go farther than what he did. This conclusion encouraged others to continue to explore the southern continent and try to go farther than what the *Adventure* and the *Resolution* did.

We feel the name *Adventure* is a worthy name for the new orbiter for several reasons. The definition of adventure is an exciting and dangerous undertaking or trip. This describes all forms of exploration. There are risks to discovering new regions, but the rewards are so great that it's worth it. *Adventure* is a good name for the space shuttle because when people go up into space, they ARE heading for an adventure!

When the sea vessel *Adventure* explored Antarctica, the crew found out more about our world. The crews of the space shuttles do the same thing. They tell us more about our world by going beyond Earth and telling us about our solar system and our universe. The ships shared a common goal; to look for new places. The sea vessel found Antarctica. Our space crew is studying the planets we know of and looking for more. Exploration isn't limited to just finding new places, but also finding out new ideas or healthy things to do.

Sea crews and space crews have to take care of themselves. The *Adventure* crew had to be careful of not getting scurvy, so they discovered that if they ate fresh fruits and onions as much as possible it might prevent them from getting sick. Space crews are studying the effects of space on their bodies. They are finding ways to keep fit and healthy while in space.

These reasons show why *Adventure* is a great name for a space shuttle, but the best reason is that it shows America's spirit, especially in exploring space. Our country was founded by people who went on adventures to learn more and to live better. From the pilgrims to the pioneers and now to the astronauts, America has always searched for adventures and took part in them, so we could learn more and make progress. There is so much to learn. We can learn more about our universe through an adventure in space aboard an orbiter named *Adventure.*

The Election of a Name

Second voyage: 1772-1775
Around Antarctica in Resolution and Adventure

The team's project compared the selection of a name for the orbiter to that of the selection of a man for President. After completing a social studies unit on electing the President, they decided to use the process for their orbiter-naming project. In their study, they learned that the candidates used different ways to persuade people to vote for them. They made speeches, traveled, and made commercials. The students set out to follow those steps to elect a name for the new orbiter.

After researching names of sea vessels, the team chose several that sounded good for a Space Shuttle. When each name was judged according to the criteria of the competition, the list was reduced to seven. Next, they polled families and friends and found that three were voted for more than any others. The three names became the candidates in their election process.

The team then divided into three parties. Each party campaigned for its name. A secret ballot vote was taken, and the name elected was *Adventure.* Because a presidential candidate's progress was reported on in newscasts, the team decided to write a newscast on the *Adventure* and its journey.

The newscast took them back in time to report on the ship's progress as if there were television newscasts in the 1770s.

■ They researched the journey of *Adventure:* its discoveries; Captain Cook; life on a ship; natural resources used on its journey; other historical events happening during that time, such as the Boston Tea Party; future events, such as the Montgolfier Brothers' proposed flight in a hot-air balloon; physical and mental conditions of the crew; and weather reports, which became more scientific after a weather study in science class.

■ They made a time line from 1772 to 1988 to determine the progress of the world and to see how important exploration was to that progress.

■ They mapped *Adventure's* journey to Antarctica and its return, and wrote a captain's log about what it would be like to be a captain of a ship.

■ The team worked in groups to write reports for the newscast. One group created the news channel number and name and the backdrop for the broadcast, which was produced using a cardboard box as a television set.

The newscast helped the students learn more about *Adventure* and what it meant in terms of exploration. They became convinced it was the perfect name for the new orbiter. The next step in the project was to convince the orbiter-naming committee.

During the 1988 election, the team saw how Michael Dukakis and George Bush used commercials to get people to vote for them. To prove that *Adventure* was a worthy name for a Space Shuttle, the team decided to make a commercial to convince the NASA committee to choose their name. Because the team had so many members, they created two commercials.

Each group worked to plan, write, and produce a commercial. One of the commercials was to appeal to people's imaginations; the other was to be a bandwagon-type commercial that emphasized how everyone thought *Adventure* was a great name.

Second voyage: 1772-1775
Around Antarctica in Resolution *and* Adventure

■ They began with the writing; next, deciding who would be in charge of props, music, special effects, and speaking parts; directing; and producing commercials that supported the name and would persuade the orbiter-naming committee to choose *Adventure.*

■ After several rehearsals, they taped the commercials. A student's father brought his camcorder to school and did the taping. When he sent the final product to the class, the team enjoyed seeing the results of their work.

The last part of a presidential election is the general election. The final step in this election would be completed by the NASA orbiter-naming committee: selecting *Adventure* as the name for OV-105.

Model for the Future

The project involved writing skills, research, deciding what things were important for it, the election process, democratic voting, public speaking, art and construction skills, acting, and teamwork.

The general outline of the project can be used for future activities in which the same process would be used when something must be chosen or researched, such as electing a class president or studying any historical event.

Calypso

Calypso. *Courtesy of The Cousteau Society, member supported, nonprofit environmental organization.*

Why *Calypso*

TOWLE ELEMENTARY SCHOOL
86 North Main Street
Newport,
New Hampshire 03773

Daniel D. Cherry
Team Coordinator
Teacher, Grade 6

TEAM MEMBERS

Joshua Archibald
Jody Barry
Roland Bedard
Charlotte Caron
Genera Clay
Sarah Corliss
Kim Cossingham
Erin Cram
Julie Fontaine
Jamie Gould
Tonia Gregory
Jayson Harris
Beth Hertzler
Michael Hughes
Lisa Leighton
Shawn McNamera
Mandy Merrill
Matthew Meunier
Toby Moore
David Nutting
Erik Palmer
Rene Patten
Maria Ploss
Shannon St. Francis
Travis Watkins
Todd Weed
Jeremy Willey

We have chosen the name *Calypso* for the OV 105. The name *Calypso* is based on Jacques Cousteau's research vessel.

The *Calypso* was originally a 360-ton YMS-Class mine sweeper that was 140 feet long and built in the United States in 1942 for the Royal Navy. After the war, the *Calypso* served as a ferry between Malta and Gozzo.

By 1951 Jacques Cousteau had assembled a working crew and began much of his research aboard the *Calypso*. The *Calypso* has been involved with many different research and explorative studies. The *Calypso* has made profile maps of the sea floor, more accurate maps of the Mediterranean Sea and other oceans. She has been involved with excavation and archaeological reconnaissance in the Aegean Sea as well as rescue attempts at sea. The *Calypso* has done research on whales, dolphins, and many other forms of sea life. From prospecting for oil to exploring the Strait of Hormuz, the *Calypso* has done it all.

The *Calypso* is the only true exploration and research vessel out of our original list of names. We feel that the name already carries a great deal of pride and respect throughout the areas of research and exploration. It would be fitting to bestow this name on the exploration and research craft of the sky, the OV 105.

We feel that America's mission in space is to help us learn about our planet, solar system, and even the universe. The *Calypso* has helped us to learn more about our own secret universe on Earth, the oceans. We also feel that America's mission in space is to look for other life forms (advanced or primitive) as well as searching other planets for resources that may be useful on Earth. We feel that the *Calypso* has done all of these things from "Sea to shining Sea" and that the *Calypso* orbiter can complete the cycle for the "spacious skies."

The *Calypso* has contributed to many inventions that have made life easier for science and man. Such things as a high definition underwater television camera and the aqualung have allowed many to join in researching the oceans. We know that the shuttle program has brought many useful inventions to mankind already and will continue to do so in the future.

We feel that *Calypso* is a good name for radio transmission because its initial consonant sounds the hard "K" sound and *Calypso* ends with a clear long "O" which can easily be distinguished at the end of a word.

A Curriculum Project

The team's project had two parts: (1) developing a classroom unit to learn more about the chosen name and the Space Shuttle, and (2) a culminating activity in which the entire class could participate.

Choosing a name was difficult. From their library research, the team compiled a list of about 10 names. Small groups supported a favorite name in papers that they presented to the class. The list was cut to three names and the debate went on as students found it hard to try to persuade people to change their minds. Finally, the name *Calypso* was chosen.

To build a unit around *Calypso,* the students investigated topic areas of the curriculum. This was another difficult task, because they did not know what could or should be taught to them. Then they figured out that teachers could help. They arranged meetings with different teachers in their school and built such a long list of ideas that it had to be cut. Considerations of money, time, and materials helped set limitations that made their activity workable. Organized into small groups, all were encouraged to pick things they would enjoy doing.

- The math group focused their lesson on large numbers and exponents. Knowing they needed to talk about big numbers because of the weight, cost, speed, and distances related to the Shuttle, they learned to use exponents so they could write numbers in a "shorter" way. "Ten billion miles could look like this 10,000,000,000 or like this 1.0×10^{10}," they found.

- The science group found a propulsion experiment in which a balloon is propelled down a string of air by pressure.

- The library and computer group helped create a list of books related to outer space and suggested that the word processor be used to type their report.

- The arts group—art, music, and physical education—had a neat lesson on sound effects. The students had to create sounds that might be in a space movie with things like wood, plastic, salt, soda, and other items to be found at home in order to learn about sound and vibration as well as how sounds can create a mood or feeling.

- A career section developed when the students could not say what they planned for their futures. Wanting to involve their parents and the community in their project, they invited guest speakers to discuss their jobs. They learned that the Shuttle program involves thousands of people besides astronauts and other NASA personnel.

- The language arts group developed creative writing topics related to the Space Shuttle and *Calypso* that offered not only serious learning, but amusement, and "sometimes spelling lists."

- The special projects group suggested building a papier-mâché model of the Shuttle and put the name *Calypso* on it. The form of the Shuttle was made with newspapers saved from the language arts unit, and donated chicken wire; the teacher provided wheat paste, and the art teacher helped them start. The entire school enjoyed the construction process.

The team felt their project was related to the name *Calypso* because the name itself has three different meanings: one definition refers to the sea nymph in Homer's *Odyssey* (language arts, reading, history); another definition is "a bog orchid bearing a single flower" (science); and the third is "improvised ballad" (the arts). Covering all the subject areas they learn in school, the name brought their entire project together.

Model for the Future

Future classroom activities based on the project seem unlimited. The almost seven-foot-tall model was to be moved to the town library for all to share. In addition to a classroom unit, there were a number of immediate spinoffs: coin and stamp collecting, interest in the Soviet shuttle program, viewing public television specials, and watching the news on television and reading newspapers to keep up with world affairs.

Nautilus

The crew of USS Nautilus *(SSN 571) stand quarters for muster as she enters New York Harbor after her transpolar voyage under the Arctic ice. OFFICIAL U. S. NAVY PHOTOGRAPH.*

Why *Nautilus*

The following papers are samples of the essays written by the third-grade team members on their choice.

JAMES MADISON
INTERMEDIATE SCHOOL
New Dover Road
Edison, New Jersey 08820

Maxine Cahn
Team Coordinator
Teacher, Grade 3

TEAM MEMBERS

Laura Adornetto
Debra Alban
Karen Axelrod
Keith Ayers
Purvi Bhagat
Kevin Boesman
Jason Brauth
Vanessa Carnovale
Alicia Gadsden
Nazmi Husenaj
Hitaishi Joshi
Nicole Lecky
Joseph Lee
Douglas Levine
Paul Meyler
Nicole Owens
Haresh Patel
Kartik Patel
David Petersen
Ellyn Poltrock
Michael Sanabria
Fariha Sheikh
Amanda Szemborski
Kelly Tyrrell

Nautilus is the best name for the OV 105. The *Nautilus* was the first nuclear powered submarine and it weighed 3,000 tons. It found a new shorter route from Japan to Europe under the ice of the North Pole. *Nautilus* is a good name for the new OV 105 because both ships go on missions of exploration and discovery. The name *Nautilus* came from a Greek word "naus", meaning " ship". The new *Nautilus* will be a ship to the stars. Both ships have well-trained, specially picked crews who are brave and confident. This new *Nautilus* will be a pathfinder just like the first *Nautilus*.

— *David Petersen*

I picked the name *Nautilus* for the OV 105 Space Shuttle. I feel that *Nautilus* is an appropriate name for the new space shuttle because the *Nautilus* was used to reach and explore the greatest depths of the unknown, just as the OV 105 will be used. The *Nautilus* had to be strong enough to withstand the tremendous pressures of the deep ocean and the OV 105 also has to be strong enough to withstand the pressures of outer space. In 1958, this American ship made history when it sailed under the ice of the North Pole from Japan to Europe. I hope that the OV 105 shuttle will also make history and have a successful journey.

It captures the spirit of America's mission in space by showing how exploration and bravery can produce new discoveries.

— *Michael Sanabria*

I think the new space shuttle should be named the *Nautilus*. The *Nautilus* is a very famous submarine in United States history. The *Nautilus* sailed under water and completed a long journey. The submarine went from the Pacific Ocean to the Atlantic Ocean. It made history on August 3, 1958 by sailing under the North Pole's ice. When the crew accomplished the journey they said, "A dream has become a reality. We have arrived."

I feel that the *Nautilus* is a wonderful name for the new spacecraft because it accomplished an amazing task. When it sailed under the ice at the North Pole it saved 4,900 miles on an underwater journey from Japan to Europe. The crew of the *Nautilus* had a dream that came true, and I think maybe the dream to visit the planets may come true. Perhaps the spaceship *Nautilus* can make history too.

—*Ellyn Poltrock*

Classroom Museum

The third-grade class embarked on a stimulating study when they sought to learn all they could about the American space program—past accomplishments and exciting possibilities—to understand its spirit and then to share their knowledge and enthusiasm with their schoolmates and families. To accomplish this objective, they transformed their classroom into a space museum.

First, they borrowed as many books as they could about ships and explorers to compile a list of names of sea vessels that they could consider for the Space Shuttle. Each student worked with a partner to scan the materials for names. The class asked family and friends for additional suggestions. They decided they could make a more educated choice after they studied the space program in depth. The nominations for a possible choice were displayed in class to refer to as the unit of study progressed.

The next research project centered on becoming knowledgeable about past space-program accomplishments. Once again, the team turned to the school and community libraries for information and to their personal collections of pictures, souvenirs, and reading material for the exhibit. An impressive time line emerged involving great amounts of math, reading, and the concept of a time line taught in social studies.

When they designed the time line, the students measured the classroom walls and decided on a scale to be used. They considered one inch for one month, but that was soon changed to two inches when the students saw the difficulty of arranging the information for years that had many missions. They also decided to illustrate only manned space flights because of limited space. For days, the classmates spent hours on the floor measuring and marking each year with two-inch months. Using rulers, yardsticks, and counting by two became part of every day's activity.

The students worked in pairs until all 28 years were completed. The manned space flights were noted with dates, astronauts' names, number of orbits, and any different or unusual accomplishments. In some cases pictures were included to enhance the appearance. The time line covered two classroom walls.

Another interesting part of their museum was a Moon-watch display. Each student charted the Moon's phases for the 28-day cycle. They also wanted to understand the possibility of future planetary exploration. Once again they worked in teams. Each team researched and reported on a different planet. Through their research, they were to decide if it would be possible to send manned spacecraft to their planet and then they were to justify their decision. As a culmination to their research, they constructed papier-mâché planets for display.

Then parents were asked to help their children design an exhibit. The results were beautiful models of future space stations, satellites, solar systems, charts on the constellations, and even an original poem.

When completed, the classroom museum was opened to the school population and the team's families. Each team member prepared a short talk about an exhibit, and visitors were treated to a guided tour. Two members designed a space crossword puzzle that was given to visitors as a souvenir.

Just one thing remained to be done—to select their name for the new orbiter. They were prepared to make an educated choice, and after reviewing the list of sea vessels, discussing their accomplishments, and relating each one to the American space program, a secret ballot was taken. *Nautilus* was the team's choice. To complete their contest entry, each team member wrote a persuasive statement on the name. Three of the essays are included in the first section of this activity.

Model for the Future

The team is especially proud that their time line will stay in the building on display. Each year, new panels will be added to show new accomplishments and it will remain a living time line.

Victory

North Hendon: snow cottages of the Boothians, *watercolor by Captain Sir John Ross, RN, from his second Arctic expedition, 1829-33. Courtesy of Scott Polar Research Institute, Cambridge, England.*

Why *Victory*

KENNEDY MIDDLE SCHOOL
721 Tomasita Avenue, NE.
Albuquerque,
New Mexico 87123

Sylvia A. Fox
Team Coordinator
Teacher of the Gifted
Grades 6-8

TEAM MEMBERS
GRADE 6

Jennifer Craig
Nando Fresquez
Shad Hernandez
Elizabeth Hinton
Jessica Todd

Victory was a specially built ship that was commanded by John Ross. This ship withstood the ice and freezing weather of the Arctic. In 1829 it made several journeys across the ice to King William Island to study the Eskimo Culture.

On the scientific side it became the first ship to reach the North Magnetic Pole. After reaching the North Magnetic Pole, John Ross was in a good position to be assigned to search for the South Magnetic Pole.

Victory is an appropriate name for a space craft because this ship was successful. It was the first ship to reach the North Magnetic Pole and study the Eskimo Culture.

Like the ship, *Victory,* the new orbiter is expecting to have a successful journey and learn more about space. The name *Victory* would represent what we are expecting this orbiter to do on all of its missions. Space shuttles that have gone into space in the past have been victorious in accomplishing the goals of their mission and so will the *Victory.*

The word *Victory* captures the spirit of America's space missions for several reasons. One mission is to acquire new knowledge about man and about how he functions in space. The ship, *Victory,* provided knowledge about the North Magnetic Pole and the Eskimo Culture. Another of America's missions in space is to conduct experiments that will contribute to man's needs on Earth and also to his ability to live in space. In learning about the Eskimo Culture, man learned how to survive in a difficult environment. The ship commanded by John Ross provided information on how to survive in a new environment. The orbiter named *Victory* would provide information on how to live and work in space.

The new orbiter's missions in space would be peaceful. The *Victory's* mission under the command of John Ross was peaceful.

The new orbiter's goal in space is to be successful and the word Victory means success or winning. Victory suggests being triumphant in accomplishing successful space missions. Victory gives the idea of conquering space mission goals. All these things bring out the spirit of America's space missions.

Traveling Through Time—Space History

From hundreds of ships—submarines, battleships, clipper ships, merchant ships, deep sea exploration ships, ice cutters—they found in library books, the team chose six names they liked and researched the ships in depth. After presenting persuasion speeches on the individual ships, the students voted for their favorite. They voted for *Victory.*

With their name selected, the team considered several projects and decided to make a history film, *Traveling Through Time—Space History.*

■ The script began with a time machine for the future. After building the machine, the main character begins his travels with the Apollo program of the 1960s, the lunar landing, and the hope it gave for future space investigations.

■ The next segment was about the Space Shuttle orbiters and their importance to space history. Each team member researched an orbiter and wrote a section for the script.

■ The film concludes in the future with the *Victory* orbiter. The final scene shows the operator of the time machine walking away after selling his invention to NASA.

■ With the script completed, the students learned the mechanics of making a film: using a storyboard; designing costumes and props; creating sound effects; preparing scenes; acting; editing; and using a camera.

An important part of their project was learning how to critique a film. The team developed the following form, "CRITIQUE, Analysis and Review," for critics to follow:

I. Visual Elements

Discuss the following and give examples from the movie that support what you say.

   A. Realism
   B. Color
   C. Light
   D. Movement
   E. Transition from scene to scene

II. Actors/Actresses

Discuss the work that each student in class did in their role for the movie.

   A. Gestures
   B. Personal involvement—interest
   C. Emotions
   D. Voice, volume, tone, speech, change in voice

III. Sound Effects

Discuss the music and sound effects used in the movie: Appropriateness (too much, too little); how they might have been improved.

IV. Write down your reactions to the film when you saw it. Discuss the overall effect, your favorite parts, your favorite lines, and discuss whether the purpose of the film is clear to the audience. Last of all, explain the purpose or purposes of this film.

In completing their evaluations, the students were severe in their self-criticism. But they also acknowledged the learning and the fun they experienced working as a team, how enjoyable it was "although doing research was not my favorite part." And after listing a host of new facts learned, another student wrote, "I really enjoyed this project because we worked together and laughed hysterically."

The climax of their project was showing their film at the Winter Fest in December 1988 to which they invited their parents, teachers, and other students.

Model for the Future

In addition to some immediate uses for the film, such as showing it to other classes with a set of questions for students to answer or making a sound effects tape to accompany the script, the team offered several suggestions for its ongoing use:

■ Show it to incoming fifth-graders as an example of what sixth-graders have done;

■ Hold a play competition between grade levels with Space Shuttles and Space History as the subject;

■ Write a play with questions at the end for different subjects;

■ Have the students make the play a musical;

■ Use the film as a motivation for other classes to learn film-making.

North Star

DR. DEE, JOHN DAVIS, AND ADRIAN GILBERT DISCUSSING N.W. PASSAGE WITH SIR FRANCIS WALSINGHAM.

Illustration from A Life of
John Davis, The Navigator
*by Clements R. Markham.
New York: Dodd, Mead &
Company, 1892. Courtesy
of Library of Congress.*

Why *North Star*

The *North Star* was a ship used by the English explorer John Davis (or Davys). John Davis was born in Sandridge (near Dartmouth), England in 1550. He was part of a group of explorers that was looking for a northwest passage to the Spice Islands.

In 1585 Davis made his first voyage with Sir Walter Raleigh to search for a northwest passage. He sailed again in 1586 and 1587 back to North America in the *North Star* searching for a passage to the Indies. Davis and his crew in the *North Star* discovered Baffin Bay, Davis Strait (named after him), Cape Farewell, Cape Dyer, and Cape Exeter. He also sailed along the west coast of Greenland. He is often known as the "Father of Arctic Discovery" for his explorations of Greenland during this time.

The name *North Star* is a good name for a spacecraft because its name is also an object in space. Navigators used it to guide their ships from early times to the present. Christopher Columbus as well as John Davis and other explorers used it to guide their ships and explorations.

The name *North Star* captures the spirit of America's mission in space because it is a guiding light. America's space program has always been a guiding light to inspire and lead the world in exploring outer space.

The new shuttle *North Star* will inspire and guide America's space mission into the 21st century. The *North Star* will guide America's scientists and engineers to build and create new space stations to help make a better world. The *North Star* will help to guide America's youth into new educational frontiers. These students today will be the scientists and leaders of the 21st century.

America's youth will be the guides into the technological and scientific realm of this new century so it seems appropriate that they should "hitch their wagon to a star". (Emerson)

EAST IREDELL
ELEMENTARY SCHOOL
400 East Elementary Road
Statesville,
North Carolina 28677

Cynthia A. Jones
Team Coordinator
Teacher of the
Learning Disabled, K-5

TEAM MEMBERS

William L. Allison (5)
Brandon Barber (4)
James K. Dew (5)
Zane Lambert (5)
Roscoe Tucker (5)

NASA – Now Aboard for Student Achievement

East Iredell's project starred five exceptional students with learning problems who led over 900 other students in a creative and motivating program in which students developed and practiced goal-setting skills. The project team was chosen because they do not often get an opportunity to lead their peers by setting goals for themselves and others.

The team began by researching and ferreting out information on various explorers and their expeditions. They decided which explorers to read more about based on the names of their ships. If a name wasn't appropriate for the new Shuttle, they discarded it. After eliminating many names, the group settled on a list of 15, then narrowed the list to five based on test criteria. The team

decided that for the name to be truly representative of the whole school, it should be decided on democratically. They presented a program to the student body in which they informed the school of the background of each ship's name and their justification for selecting it. In a school-wide election the school chose the name *North Star* as the most representative of their goal-setting program.

The project was divided into two parts. One dealt with the five-man research team and the second was an outgrowth of their efforts. As the team shared their excitement and involvement in the contest with their friends, other students and teachers asked to be a part of the project. From this growing interest, they adopted a school-wide space theme for the 1988-89 school year.

Using titles that reflected the space program, a Chain of Achievement was organized. Students could climb this chain by setting an academic or behavioral goal for each grading period. The Chain of Achievement was arranged so that as students climbed the chain, they rose higher in rank and status.

Level 5 - Astronaut

↑

Level 4 - Space Officer

↑

Level 3 - Mission Specialist

↑

Level 2 - Ground Crew

↑

Level 1 - Recruit

Classroom teachers monitored the individual progress of their students as they worked toward reaching their goals. Students who met their goals were "promoted" in small promotion ceremonies at the end of each grading period. One student from each class who set an exemplary standard in reaching his or her goal was chosen as a Star Student. These students received Star Student T-shirts purchased by the STPA (parent-teacher organization). Thirty-five Star Students were chosen each grading period, thereby giving many children the opportunity to be awarded this special title.

By year's end, students who set and met five goals would achieve the rank of Astronaut.

To emphasize the importance of the Chain of Achievement, during the orbiter-naming project special space-related activities were carried out each month.

From the beginning, parental involvement was a vital part of Operation NASA. They assisted their children by monitoring their progress at school and supporting them at home. They also contributed materials to be used for the Spaceship East Week in October. A 13-foot x 8-foot mural of a Shuttle in flight was donated by parents to the school and now hangs in a prominent location. A businessman, with no school connections whatsoever, was so enthusiastic about the school's project that he donated his entire collection of space mission patches

to the school library. The local radio station kept the community-at-large informed of the activities through the Iredell County Schools Radio Show. The local paper, *The Statesville Record and Landmark,* featured the East Iredell project in a Sunday edition. All in all, the NASA project at East Iredell was major community news in 1988.

Preliminary observations at the time their orbiter-naming project was submitted showed exceptional student interest and a high rate of goal completion by the entire student body. Teachers also reported a renewed interest among students in space and science.

Model for the Future

The team feels this project would adapt perfectly to any school setting from the smallest rural communities to large metropolitan areas. Although it is a school-wide program, it is implemented in the classroom on a one-to-one basis by teacher and child. It can be as large or as small as the school wants to make it, but the goal-setting component remains effective and constant throughout.

"Ideals are like stars. You will not succeed in touching them with your hands; but like the seafaring man, you choose them as your guides, and following them, you will reach your destiny." (Carl Schurz)

Pathfinder

USS **Pathfinder.** *Courtesy of National Oceanic and Atmospheric Administration, Department of Commerce.*

Why *Pathfinder*

The name we have chosen for the OV 105 is *Pathfinder.* The sea vessel after which it is named is the *Pathfinder* built in 1899 for the Coast and Geodetic Survey.

The *Pathfinder* has an interesting history. The discovery of gold in Southeastern Alaska in 1882 made it necessary to survey the coast of Alaska. The Klondike gold rush in 1898 brought the Survey's new 168 foot *Pathfinder* to Alaskan waters to survey Northern Sound and the Fox Islands in the Aleutians.

Several students presented individual reasons for the selection of the name:

I believe the name *Pathfinder* is a very good name because our whole history deals with pathfinders who explored the sea, the land, and now space . . . . Pathfinders are sea, land and space explorers. Ships found paths across the oceans. On land the pioneer wagons found paths to where they wanted to settle. In space the shuttle finds paths to the stars and planets . . . . I think *Pathfinder* is an appropriate name because the word "orbit" means "path" and the shuttle orbiters are exploring ships that find paths in space. . . . A pathfinder is a person who discovers a way or makes out a new route. . . . A pathfinder can also be a vehicle such as a sailing ship or an orbiter. . . . The Pioneers of the Oregon Trail were pathfinders. Our space explorers are the "pathfinders of the stars." . . . *Pathfinder* is a name that makes you think of discovery. Pathfinders make the way for others to reach for new frontiers in space and science. Astronauts make new discoveries for us on on their missions in space. . . . Knowing little or nothing of what lay beyond, explorers and pioneers became pathfinders. The spirit and imagination of yesterday's pathfinders help us now to meet the challenge of exploring space. The name *Pathfinder* captures the spirit of America's mission in space!

Pathfinders

"From the Oregon Trail to the Orbiter Trail" introduces the sixth-grade team's project, a coloring calendar called *Pathfinders.*

To select the name, the class worked in six crews. Each crew decided upon one name; the six names were presented to the class, and *Pathfinder* was chosen. For a project idea, the class voted to design a calendar to promote and encourage interest in the local and national history of our pioneering past (Oregon Trail Monument) and space exploration (Orbiter-Naming Program and space missions).

The calendar illustrates the name *Pathfinder* in art, words, and song to express how man's imagination has led him along paths to discovery and knowledge. The team decided on this project for two reasons:

CHURCHILL
ELEMENTARY SCHOOL
3451 Broadway
Baker, Oregon 97814

Mrs. Wes A. Brown
Team Coordinator
Teacher, Grade 6

TEAM MEMBERS

Trisha Bootsma
Melinda Cameron
Aimee Chapek
Jeff Creemer
Shondo Dailey
Jeff Dillman
Cory Dopp
Carrie Edison
Gretchen Gast
J. R. Grover
David Hanley
Jake Henry
Jacquelin Leavell
Joe Lethlean
Trudi Martinez
Howard Miller
Jeremy Myers
Eric Nichols
Christopher Parker
Rusty Parrish
Nick Profitt
Dennis Rexroad
Colleen Rouse
Robert Slinker
Ken Smith
Torianna Vinson
Arthur Willman
Clint Woydziak

- To promote local and regional interest in and enthusiasm for the development of the National Historic Oregon Trail Interpretive Center near their community of Baker. The center was scheduled to open in spring 1991.

- To share their interest in and enthusiasm for the new orbiter and space exploration. The new orbiter also was scheduled for completion in spring 1991.

Because of current interest in the community for the development of the nearby Oregon Trail Interpretive Center on Flagstaff Hill, the team wanted to develop a project connected to the center and the historic value of the trail. The few paths that are left of the Oregon Trail, which crossed the state from Baker to Oregon City, are being preserved to educate Americans about this historically important segment of the trail.

To develop their calendar, the students divided the class into three theme groups—Ocean Pathfinder, Pioneer Pathfinder, and Space Pathfinder. Completing their project involved the following activities:

- Studying past accomplishments of explorers and pioneers in history;

- Exploring relationships and reasons for man's vast westward movement and reasons for man's mission in space;

- Exploring humanity's impact on the environment;

- Issuing invitations to local historians to share their knowledge and to students of other grades to contribute art work to the calendar;

- Designing calendar and organizing printing;

- Arranging distribution by students, parents, and community businesses (proceeds from the calendar were donated to the Oregon Trail National Monument Committee for use in promoting the National Historic Oregon Trail Interpretive Center at Flagstaff Hill).

The team planned to enter the project in the annual Niftee Learning Olympics and Fair. Niftee (Nurturing Intercommunity Family Teamwork and Excellence in Education) is an annual event that provides opportunity for students in Baker County and their families to be recognized for their achievements in education.

Model for the Future

The students felt that the value of working on the project was best expressed by a class member in answer to the question, "Why is NASA offering the opportunity for young people to name the new orbiter and why should we participate?" The response:

"So we can expand our imaginations and be excited about space exploration." They also felt that by participating in the national Orbiter-Naming Program they became actively and meaningfully involved in their own community project of local and national interest.

As an outcome of their project, the class proposed a potential project list for future classroom and school activities:

- Help organize school field trips via shuttle bus to Oregon Trail Monument Visitor's Center;

- Propose and design footpath/bike trail from Baker to Oregon Trail Monument (five miles) for walkers, joggers, and bikers;

- Promote tourism through student-designed travel brochures and newsletters;

- Create and participate in dramas, plays, and musical productions at the Oregon Trail Interpretive Center;

- Out of the Past - Into the Future! Proposal for the year 2000: Develop Spaceport USA Northwest Museum at Flagstaff Hill site.

Horizon

Horizon. *Courtesy of Scripps Institution of Oceanography, University of California— San Diego, La Jolla, California.*

Why *Horizon*

WESTERN HILLS ELEMENTARY SCHOOL
400 Phenix Avenue
Cranston,
Rhode Island 02920

Marilyn I. Remick
Team Coordinator
Enrichment Teacher
Grades 4-6

TEAM MEMBERS
GRADE 6

Dennis Del Barone
Kelly Creighton
Brian Germanowski
Robert Giardino
Amy Nichols
Stephen Pantano
Adam Rappoport
Jaclyn Sabatino
Corey Ventetuolo

Our team has decided that the best name for OV 105 is *Horizon.* It was a former Navy sea-going tug that was built in 1944. It was converted to an oceanographic research ship in 1948.

Following World War II, the government supported oceanographic research at universities and institutions such as Scripps Institute of Oceanography, which operated the *Horizon* as part of its educational and research programs until 1969. It was used to investigate the composition of the ocean bottom, the properties of waves and currents, and the interaction of water and atmosphere.

We think *Horizon* is appropriate for a spacecraft because it reflects government support for research and education. It is a good name for a spacecraft because we are always aiming for new horizons in space exploration. The space shuttles always work on the edges of our knowledge of space the way a horizon is the edge of our world. The shuttle challenges and moves beyond the earth's horizon physically as well as intellectually and emotionally.

In a NASA publication, "America's Spaceport," it said, "as science and technology move forward to new horizons, the men and women of America's Spaceport will be challenged as never before to keep pace." We believe the orbiter *Horizon* will help capture this spirit of America's mission in space.

The *Horizon* is an appropriate name because it symbolizes the new achievements and discoveries around the corner. It suggests the astronauts' exploration of the vast area of our universe. Human curiosity and global problems demand that we look into the future and set goals. *Horizon* is a name which will inspire people around the world.

TIME, December 31, 1992

The team, after many hours of brainstorming and research, decided to create a future issue of TIME magazine about the first flight of the orbiter *Horizon.* They chose it as a project because magazines print current information. People reading the articles learn new information that was once part of the future—over the horizon—but is becoming reality. Magazines and newspapers operate on the horizon of information and bring it to the public.

The students liked the idea of being investigative reporters and broadening their personal horizons by doing something they had never done: taking the role of magazine reporters and editors and bringing into form the shape of a famous magazine.

The team took a field trip on a boat called *Envirolab* to learn more about oceanographic research. They were allowed to conduct different experiments

and handle some marine specimens to get the feeling of doing research and understanding what it must be like for astronauts to conduct experiments on board the orbiter. The entire class enjoyed an evening field trip to the Seagrave Observatory to see how telescopes work and how astronomers observe the stars.

For their magazine they picked the first flight of the orbiter *Horizon* because it is not part of the past, yet not too far into the future. They could see it "coming just over the horizon." As *Horizon* enters space, we will get more immediate knowledge than from a Space Station, which takes longer than a Shuttle to put up and produce information. In contrast, information about the new Shuttle is current, like material in an actual TIME magazine. People who read the team's articles about the new orbiter would be excited by what is going to happen in the immediate future.

Team members were careful when dividing up the article and activity assignments to be sure they covered all disciplines. One reason they picked a TIME magazine project was the magazine's format, which lent itself very nicely to the approach because it includes music, health, science, etc.

■ The team elected two editors to keep track of assignments. Both editors and reporters went back to the libraries for information on their respective topics. In their research, the team had to learn facts about space technology in order to comprehend complex concepts and apply that knowledge when they created the activities and advertisements. They also had to analyze many parts of the orbiter's design and routine in order to complete their articles.

■ They found that the advertisements, art work, and activities challenged their imaginations and gave them a new approach to learning about favorite space topics.

■ They found they enjoyed the role of adult reporters on a real life magazine and learned a lot about how a magazine is put together, especially meeting publication deadlines.

■ They kept track of individual contributions to the project with a bulletin board that had a picture of an orbiter. Each student had a smaller orbiter with squares which were filled in as a contribution was submitted. This innovative recordkeeping device was a good motivator because team members were recognized for their participation.

As each team member turned in his or her rough draft, three volunteer members typed them on the school's word processors. Final copy was then assembled. Copies were distributed to the other classrooms so those students could participate in evaluating the project as well as enjoy the activities included. Next, the team sampled the student body to see how many would enjoy participating in a similar mock magazine-writing simulation. Answer: 78%.

Model for the Future

It was especially exciting for the team to think of saving their product and comparing it to the real, future Launch of OV-105 issue of TIME to see how close they came to their predictions. Thus, they thought the project a fine model for future classrooms because it would inspire them to strive for their own vision of a magazine of the future.

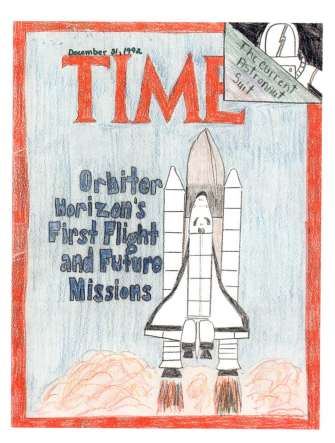

Victory

FRONT VIEW of the VICTORY, in FELIX HARBOUR.

Illustration from Last Voyage of Capt. Sir John Ross *by Robert Huish. London, 1836. Courtesy of Library of Congress.*

Why *Victory*

*KAYSVILLE
ELEMENTARY SCHOOL
50 North 100 East
Kaysville, Utah 84037*

*Virginia B. Cate
Team Coordinator
Enrichment Aide*

*TEAM MEMBERS
GRADES 5-6*

*Jacob Allen (6)
Justin Allen (5)
Nathan Burdsal (5)
Brian Hyde (5)*

The *Victory* was part of a three-ship expedition which set sail for the Arctic in 1829. Sir John Ross was commander of the small exploration fleet and was accompanied by his nephew, Capt. James Clark Ross. They were attempting to find a northwest passage, but unfortunately their vessels became frozen in arctic ice. These early sailor-scientists did not waste their time, however. While waiting for a thaw, they studied the Eskimos and recorded much about their habits and lifestyle.

The name *Victory* denotes overcoming hard challenges. *Victory* is an appropriate name for the new space shuttle because it represents our country's successes in the space program and the many hard challenges which have been met and conquered.

Though the ship *Victory* was not able to complete this mission, it served a great purpose. It was on arctic expeditions such as this one that the great explorer, James Clark Ross, received his training. He later discovered the Ross Ice Shelf and made many other significant scientific contributions.

When the horrible tragedy happened with the *Challenger,* most people all over the world and even in the United States thought that the space program was over for the U.S.A. But, when *Discovery* was launched and we had another victory, they changed their minds.

Victory brings to mind "winning." *Victory* also says that the United States space program has many triumphs yet to come as technology grows and we learn more about space.

Victory in Space, A Board Game

The team's project was conducted in the Enrichment Room as part of the Schoolwide Enrichment Model at Kaysville Elementary School. Students attend the enrichment program for one half-hour twice a week.

First, the students researched the names of sea vessels and, as they found names of interesting ships that might be appropriate for a spacecraft, recorded them on the board. Next, they found definitions for the words that were the names. They also listed synonyms for the words and any kind of image a word brought to mind. With all of this information on the board, they voted unanimously for *Victory*.

The team chose a trivia game for their project because it would help them and anyone who plays it to learn about the space program while having fun. Victory in Space is a board game that deals with both the new generation of explorers in space and the older generations of great explorers. Players orbit all the planets on the board and the Moon, visit the Space Station, overcome dangers, reap rewards, and return to Earth. The students felt that everyone who plays the game wins because of the many things learned.

After selecting four areas of knowledge for the trivia questions, the students listed the things they had to accomplish:

■ Decide how the game would be played and write the rules.

■ Research and write trivia questions.

■ Make up dangers and rewards.

■ Construct game board and other equipment.

Each member of the team researched a different area and wrote questions about it, wrote a list of dangers and rewards, and drew his ideas for a game board.

To devise the game board and rules, team members pooled ideas of other favorite games they had played. Once started, ideas seemed to roll. Each student drew some possibilities for the way the game board should look. A member drew a preliminary plan with his ideas, then they played the game, evaluated the board, and made necessary changes. This process was used more than once. Making up the game was a team effort, also. Two team members worked on drawing and coloring the board, while the other two measured and cut cards for the questions, etc. The final result is an exciting learning tool for their classrooms and school.

■ The object of Victory in Space is to orbit each spatial body on the board, land on Space Station sometime during the game, and return to Earth. The winner is the player who accomplishes this first.

■ **Players:** 2 to 6, ages 8 to adult. Teams also may play.

■ Questions are color-coded by the four subjects (at least 50 in each category):
Green   Planets and the Solar System
Red   Milestones in Space
Blue   Great Explorations of the Past
Yellow   Astronauts and Space Travel

■ **Equipment:**

1 game board	30 Danger cards
6 markers of different colors	30 Reward cards
1 die	36 Successful Orbit cards
Trivia cards with 4 questions each	(6 for each spatial body)
6 Space Station cards	

Model for the Future

The students plan to continue to learn about the space program and to write new questions periodically.

"It is almost like something magic when students begin to create something that will teach other people. Their own perception of the teaching-learning process is changed.

"Students should be encouraged to create games or any other tools which will help make learning any subject more interesting. The entire classroom atmosphere revitalizes when such projects are initiated."

Trieste

Bathyscaph Trieste *entering
water. OFFICIAL U. S.
NAVY PHOTOGRAPH.*

Why *Trieste*

WESTFORD
ELEMENTARY SCHOOL
Brookside Road
Westford, Vermont 05494

Kurt A. Sherman
Team Coordinator
Instructor, Grade 5,
and Young Astronaut
Group Leader

TEAM MEMBERS
GRADES 3, 5-7

Emmy Balon (6)
Nashua Birnholz (6)
Meghan Bress (7)
Erin Delorme (6)
Jodie Drinkwine (5)
Seth Holmes (7)
Courtney Sherman (3)
Christie Siegriest (6)

The Westford Elementary School team suggested the name *Trieste* for many reasons. The group began with 20 possibilities, but voted unanimously for the final choice. Their unanimity made it clear to them that *Trieste* is the perfect name for the next Space Shuttle.

The team spent a tremendous amount of time exploring possible names, researching potential leads, assembling a mock-up of the craft, and compiling important facts about their choice. From this work emerged *Trieste* "de profundis."

Both the *Trieste* of the 1950s and 60s and the Space Shuttles of the 1980s and 90s are vehicles used to expand the knowledge of the human race. Both are unique: The bathyscaphe descends to the deepest trenches on the planet to give views of an underwater world unseen for millions of years; the Shuttle gives humanity the ability to extend knowledge to even further reaches in space.

Similarities between the original *Trieste* and the Space Transportation System (STS) are many:

■ Both craft explore little-visited areas of inner/outer space.

■ Although *Trieste* is an undersea craft, its basic design is that of an atmospheric vehicle. Its gasoline tanks serve as an "inflatable" and its sphere as the "gondola."

■ Both ships depend on airtight/pressurized sections for passenger survival.

■ Mechanical robotic arms are adapted to both craft to complete outside tasks.

■ Both ships are used for complex and dangerous missions of discovery.

■ Unique "return to base" features are found on both. The *Trieste* uses gasoline as a bouyancy device (30% lighter than H_2O.) The Shuttle uses thermal tiles/blankets to survive atmospheric friction when entering Earth's atmosphere.

■ Both ships are semi reusable. *Trieste* sheds metal ballast in the form of BB-sized pellets when the ship wants to surface or trim; the STS sheds its ET and SRBs to escape the surface of the planet.

■ Although both ships appear quite large, the crew compartment of both is quite cramped. The *Trieste* has a sphere of only six feet in diameter, while the somewhat larger Shuttle is still cramped for seven astronauts over a week's time.

■ Communication between ships and people on the surface of the planet is necessary for the occupants aboard to complete missions successfully.

■ Safety of design and redundancy in systems have been put into both craft.

■ An international effort has gone into both craft. The *Trieste* was built in Italy, designed by a Swiss engineer, created for the French, but eventually sold to the United States. The Shuttle was built in the United States, carries aloft payloads made by other nations, gives flight experience to other countries' astronauts, and will be used to construct a multinational Space Station.

The *Trieste* was a revolutionary design, using the best technology of its day to perform difficult but essential missions of exploration and experimentation. It extends the edge of human knowledge. This also is the role of the STS. The *Trieste* was created and used with the involvement of many nations, just as the United States itself was settled and molded by the contribution of many nations, many cultures.

"By adopting the name *Trieste* the United States will take a small step toward recognizing what space itself must be the setting for; a place of international peace and a pathway toward worlds waiting to be explored."

Undersea Mission

After constructing a mock-up of the *Trieste,* the team planned and carried out a simulated mission to the bottom of the Pacific Ocean. After taking water temperature samples along the way, an ocean floor sample was taken with a robotic arm when on the bottom.

The mission was scheduled for an hour, and at the end the team was only three minutes off the timetable. Mission personnel had two to a team:

■ The bathyscaphe pilot guided the *Trieste* to the sea floor by remaining in the mock-up for one hour. Assuming a descent rate average of 3 ft/sec, the group calculated a diving depth of 10,800 ft. The pilot monitored blood pressure and temperature, made a communication and robotic-system check, and had a "free time" (music) period. Gathering an ocean floor specimen involved the other teams.

■ The video technician (vid-tech) was housed in a large cardboard box through which peered the lens of a video camera; her job was to guide the robotic arm to the specimen, but not directly to the pilot. Her communications link was the transfer crew.

■ The transfer crew relayed information out of the room with written commands to the communication technician (comm-tech).

■ The comm-tech used a walkie-talkie to communicate commands, clearly and concisely, to the pilot.

Communication was important, and each team was dependent on the others. They practiced their roles, nautical language, and using the robot, and discovered that following orders was part of the project. The students were quite satisfied with the results. They were accurate in some predictions (they thought an hour inside a box would be tough for the pilot, and about half-way through the time schedule, she did start to mumble to herself) and experienced some small-systems failures (blood pressure cuff).

Model for the Future

"Does this project have potential for future use in a classroom? You bet! Our school represents a small-scale, country school approach to completing a project. We came up with an excellent idea, used local resources effectively, spent little money, involved parents and other school officials in its completion, and had a great deal of enjoyment completing it.

"This project required only large boxes, a video camera and tape, a toy robot (purchased for $15) and seven dedicated young people. These components could be duplicated in any classroom in the United States (or for that matter, most of our planet!)

"And the end result would be a challenge met, a new sense of cooperative learning and teamwork and a furthering of education toward adult life. But perhaps the greatest benefit would be FUN FOR KIDS!"

Deepstar

Deepstar *being launched from its support ship. Courtesy of Oceanic Division, Westinghouse Electric Corporation, Annapolis, Maryland.*

Why *Deepstar*

Even before our school voted and chose the *Deepstar* for the name of the new orbiter, its name had several strong points that orbiter names should have. The *Deepstar* name would be an easy name to say for young kids, radio and television announcers, and for people of other countries. It is easy to spell and would look good on the side of an orbiter. After being easy to say and look at, the word *Deepstar* itself sounds like exploring . . a shiny star . . . ! Just imagine, an orbiter floating silently *deep* in space. The words that make up the name *Deepstar* are good public relations words. We learned the importance of names to represent vessels of discovery when we were choosing ships and campaigning for them.

There are many amazing similarities between the NASA orbiter and the *Deepstar*, similarities that are important. The *Deepstar* was a small submersible manufactured by the Undersea Division of Westinghouse Electric Corporation and Captain Jacques-Yves Cousteau. Westinghouse, not just a mere refrigerator-seller, began production plans for the *Deepstar* with Cousteau in France in 1963. It was a good match of public companies and research, like NASA's program. The craft was small, it held only three people, a pilot and two scientists. Space vehicles during the sixties were not much larger than this vessel; quarters on orbiters are still cramped!

It took a long time to build and, like the Shuttle program, the *Deepstar* had material and mechanical problems. There was even an "O"-ring problem that caused the mission problems. The rings that sealed the sphere's hatch to the outside were problems. The right material for the outside, titanium, was used after a lot of experiments on metals. The shuttles have had many adjustments of materials to use for the outside.

The mission of the *Deepstar* was to explore "where man had never been before." Jacques Cousteau felt that it was important to really see the undersea world and record what was seen. The mission of NASA is to explore the world above and record it too. In the *Deepstar*, men were drifting, self-propelled under the pressure of the water. In an orbiter, they were drifting weightless, controlled by the force of gravity. Both NASA orbiters and *Deepstar* got men around in a hostile environment to learn about living there and returned them safely to our earth. The ground support of NASA Control and the sea support of Cousteau's *Calypso* made safe travel more possible for the men.

It is also important to think about Jacques Cousteau. He developed a love for the sea and wanted to see if humans could stay under water for periods of time. He launched several experiments to do this, just like NASA! After winning an election to the French Academy this year, Cousteau heads out on a trip around the world to study how other people treat and use the sea. He has used his sea vessels, including *Deepstar* for peaceful studies of

ROBERT REID
ELEMENTARY SCHOOL
210 Seventh Street
Cheney, Washington 99004

Jacqueline E. Lyons
Team Coordinator
Teacher, Grade 6

TEAM MEMBERS

Stephanie Golden
Chris Grace
Chris Haigh
Chloe Houser
Noah Skocilich
Sandra Snow

the undersea world. What a great way to honor him and his exploration and the contributions to mankind!

The spirit of Cousteau's peaceful, careful, persistent visits deep into the sea matches the spirit of the Orbiter 105's future challenge; careful, peaceful learning about space. Cousteau worked hard to train his crew well and also, the astronauts have been trained well.

Because of these things, we think *Deepstar* is the "shuttle of a new generation"; exploring new frontiers of learning, where no man has been before, with brave astronauts, just like the saucernauts of the 1960's. While they were training for their first *Deepstar* mission, the saucernauts saw the 2-man Gemini mission on TV. They saw how much the space travelers were the same as they were.

We can just hear the announcement, "The *Deepstar* is ready to launch!" and NASA astronauts and Cousteau saucernauts will both have traveled on a vessel of discovery called *Deepstar!*

Two Media Experiences, Television and Newspaper

The team divided their project into two parts. In each, they tried to involve students of their school and students from Eastern Washington University. In Phase I, they conducted a campaign to inform students about the NASA Orbiter-Naming Program and the students helped the team choose the name. In Phase II, they created a school-wide newspaper filled with games, lots of information, and advertising about some fun space products related to *Deepstar*.

Phase I, National Shipographic Game Show Special, *Name That Orbiter!*

The team conducted a campaign to tell students about the program so they could vote for one of five choices when they voted for the President and Vice President. Team members played the roles of the captains of the ships and wrote a persuasive script for videotaping, with appropriate costumes (leased by the university drama department) and accents. They did their show in a TV studio at the college campus on a set they designed. The videotape was shown to two university classes. Over 50 notes from the college students gave the team valuable feedback. The last step was to show the tape to students in their school with a voters' pamphlet for each. The 3rd,- 4th-, 5th-, and 6th-graders voted in booths for the President, Vice President, and one of the five ships. On National Election Day, George Bush, Dan Quayle, and *Deepstar* were elected.

Phase II, *The NASA Times,*
Thursday, February 15, 1992

Each team member was an editor for a section of the newspaper, responsible for articles and where they would fit in the paper. They told the story of the election of the *Deepstar* and wrote of what they had learned and their other learnings and ideas about the space program. Everyone served as both reporter and writer for his or her beat. There were editorials, features on the Shuttle and space lifestyles of the future, and a TV schedule. A page for parents included recollections of space when they were growing up and two recipes, Comet Cake and Star Clusters.

When the paper was printed, it was distributed to students, parents, the Eastern Washington University Education Department, and local newspapers.

Model for the Future

As a model for use in other classrooms, either phase of the project would be easily adaptable to use in classrooms of varied size, age, and focus. A newspaper could be focused on any NASA topic, including student experiments, discoveries, or small rocket launches. Student learnings are purposefully recorded in newspaper form for a wide audience. The availability of newspaper computer programs is reasonable for many classes, but such a program is not required to complete a school newspaper. Videotaped newscasts or other types of television presentations also have the capacity to reflect learnings purposefully to an audience outside of the classroom. Although this project was completed in a television studio, the studio may simply be the classroom, and less sophisticated video equipment used. Slide shows or live telecasts also could be performed with the same learning benefits. Many NASA-related topics could be shared with larger audiences with the videotaped program format, from dramatic to more formal presentations.

Calypso

Jacques Cousteau's Calypso *at anchor, Key West, Florida, prior to undertaking a variety of oceanographic and weather experiments for NASA in cooperation with Texas A & M University, 1974. NASA photo.*

Why *Calypso*

HAMILTON
ELEMENTARY SCHOOL
1111 South Seventh Street
La Crosse, Wisconsin 54601

Alyce J. Wehrenberg
Team Coordinator
Teacher, Grade 5

TEAM MEMBERS, GRADES 4-5

Andrew Bottner (4)
Sarah Clemence (4)
Lindsey Kirk (4)
Ethan Mutz (5)
Tricia Nissalke (4)
Leah Palmer (5)

We chose the *Calypso* as our name for the OV 105 because the orbiter will soon be going on many voyages as the *Calypso* has already done. The *Calypso* has been used to explore the ocean, discover different things, and teach mankind about many things in our changing environment. Under the direction of Captain Jacques Cousteau and his sons, Philippe and Jean-Michel, the *Calypso* travels around the world by sea, hoping to learn more things about the mysteries of our oceans. The crew of the *Calypso* also want to make mankind more aware of plant and animal life in the seas.

The *Calypso* was built in 1942. In 1950, it was the most up-to-date research ship afloat. Some voyages have taken the *Calypso* and its crew to the Red Sea as well as to all of the earth's oceans. Once the *Calypso* actually went around the world. Its first cruise was taken in 1951 to the Red Sea and later to explore some of the Spice Islands. The longest cruise it ever took was from February of 1967 to September of 1970 when it went around the world. That cruise was around 140,000 nautical miles long. On that cruise they shot about 24 films for television and a few underwater movies. The speed of the *Calypso* is from 10 to 10 1/2 knots. The gear it carries includes about 20 scuba outfits, underwater scooters, 2 minisubmarines, rafts, lifeboats, and ultrasonic telephone (used by deep-sea divers to communicate with each other and with the ship), tape recorders, and underwater microphones.

Therefore, we decided that the *Calypso* would be a good name for the OV 105 because, like the sea-going *Calypso,* it will carry important research equipment to study space. Also, like the *Calypso,* the OV 105 will be able to teach—using television and film—what life is like in space. It will bring space closer to us, just as Jacques Cousteau's *Calypso* has brought life in the sea closer to all of us today.

A Three-part Project

As a group, the team decided to include not only a written explanation of their plan to dispose of space garbage and space junk (a future problem facing all of the world's space explorers), but also a few fun activities for students that are related to what they learned while studying and investigating research material.

Part 1

Because they picked the name *Calypso,* the team felt that making a detailed, labeled drawing of the ship would be appropriate. To add usefulness and a degree of challenge for other children, they made the large drawing into a pliable puzzle that could be put together easily by most elementary students.

Part 2

The project's second part involved words the team researched when learning about the *Calypso* and its history. They developed a Word Find that elementary students would enjoy completing as an added vocabulary challenge.

Part 3

Their third project idea involved the future space problem of disposing of the tons of space garbage and junk that would quickly accumulate by people working in space. With numerous Space Shuttle trips into space to supply all types of future missions with survival needs and tools of exploration and discovery as well as defense, weather, and communication satellites, humanity will need some environmentally safe and economically reasonable means to dispose of unrecyclable materials in space.

The students' first step was to identify what they felt should be included in the plan for disposal. They divided space garbage and space junk into two categories, liquid and solid wastes. Under liquid waste would be unrecyclable chemical waste that could not be repurified in space. Also included would be body fluid waste and liquid cleansing wastes. Solid wastes would include unrecyclable food wastes, containers, clothing, solid body wastes, unreusable experimentation apparatus, and irrepairable space equipment, satellites, and vehicles of all sorts.

The next step was to investigate ways to collect and process the accumulated garbage. The nation has not had to face a large-scale problem of space garbage disposal, so little has been written about the problem. Therefore, the team brainstormed the present system of garbage disposal on Earth to see what could be done in relationship to space garbage disposal. They decided that, in space, they would need from one to several large compactors that would reduce the volume of the refuse collected by their future proposed space garbage shuttles. These would transport, as needed, the space garbage from Spacelabs and various space vehicles. Once collected, it would be compacted into smaller cubic-size units to be shuttled for disposal. The liquid waste would be put into sealed containers to be collected also for routine disposal.

This plan would have to be environmentally safe and economically reasonable. When enough space garbage and junk had been collected and processed adequately, they would send a special shuttle to the upper edges of Earth's atmosphere or to another planet's atmosphere. Here, the processed cubes and containers of solid and liquid waste would be jettisoned into the atmosphere to a point where they would react with the heat and friction of entry and burn up completely, leaving no toxic residue to pollute the planet below.

Because the team felt this will be a serious problem facing space exploration of the future, they wanted to see if they could somehow help future scientists come up with some possible solutions to the pollution of space. They feel their plan would be safe for space and Earth's environment.

Just as *Calypso* and its crew have explored the oceans in various ways and places to help mankind recognize our vast resources and understand the hidden world below Earth's surface, the team also recognizes the need to explore space for future generations. Just as *Calypso* and its crews of scientists and explorers are trying to awaken all mankind to the dangers of polluting our environment on Earth by poisoning our waters and clean air, the team sees that humanity must concern itself with pollution in space beyond Earth. One way to help solve this future problem of space garbage is to plan ahead for ways to dispose of it in a safe environmental way.

Model for the Future

Other students in the school can benefit by the project as they read about it, manipulate the puzzle pieces of the *Calypso,* and enjoy working copies of the Word Find. As they read the proposal for preventing pollution in space, they can be thinking about possible solutions to space problems that will continue to arise as humans get further involved in space exploration and discovery. All children of the world need to be concerned about pollution not only on this planet, but on other unexplored planets and all of space. Our future depends on our survival in an environmentally safe universe.

Future projects can develop from this one; other children can also come up with good ideas, develop plans to help clean up our planet, write to important people to voice their concerns about cleaning up our planet, and begin, in their own neighborhoods and cities, with small cleanup and recyling projects. If enough children show concern for the environment, they can be effective in getting the attention of adults and government leaders, who can then pass laws and legislation to help improve our planet's environment.

Resolution

Resolution, *watercolor by*
William Hodges. Courtesy of
National Maritime Museum,
Greenwich, London.

Why *Resolution*

NORTHSIDE
ELEMENTARY SCHOOL
Sixth and Washington
Lander, Wyoming 82520

Patsy B. Bailey
Team Coordinator
Teacher, Grades 5-6

TEAM MEMBERS
GRADE 6

Tara Baldwin
Chris McDonald
Jason Milburn
Shannon Quinn
Michael Trevino
Jason Trimmer
Jerry Tucker

The *Resolution* was a sister ship of *Discovery* and *Adventure* commanded by James Cook. Cook sailed in waters known to others, but he sailed farther, pushing beyond those known routes, facing unknown dangers as he carried out orders given by England. James Cook's voyage added to the knowledge of our planet. This is just like our astronauts going into space where others have gone yet adding to the knowledge of our universe today. He was known to sail with secret orders just as the crew of the *Atlantis* did.

We think *Resolution* will be a good name for the next space shuttle because the word "resolution" can mean strong will and determination. Strong will and determination describe the spirit of America perfectly. America is always trying new and different things. After *Challenger* blew up, we didn't give up our quest to challenge space. America's technology was able to locate and resolve the problems which caused that tragedy. The determination of those involved in the space program to get another shuttle into space resulted in the successful missions of *Discovery* and *Atlantis* in 1988. Man's will to overcome difficulties has caused research that will lead to the development of better and safer spacecraft.

Resolution seemed an excellent name for James Cook's ship. He was a man of strong will and determination whose goal was "not only to go farther than anyone had done before but as far as possible for man to go." Our missions in space reflect that goal. We believe that the *Resolution* (OV 105) will take our astronauts not only as far as man has already gone, but further.

The Many Meanings of Resolution

After choosing the name *Resolution* for OV-105, the team began looking at the meaning of the word. They were familiar with the resolutions that people make for January 1, but found it to be just one of many meanings. For their project they resolved to explore the unfamiliar meanings of the word.

To help them understand the other meanings, the team brainstormed activities that would give them various associated experiences. They also decided to include the residents of the Wyoming State Training School (WSTS) in appropriate activities. The WSTS is the facility for the mentally handicapped of Wyoming and an important part of their community. They also resolved to exchange visits between the schools and to be helpers in the Summer Olympics to be held in Lander in the summer 1989. Many people in the community helped the team with information and technical assistance.

Because a resolution is a democratic decision made by a group with a common goal, they resolved to agree on their activities, to share the work, to do their best, to involve members of the community, to attend every meeting, to listen and to accept each others' ideas, to respect people's rights, to learn more

about spacecraft and space travel, to learn about heavenly bodies, to learn about some of the space missions and patches, and to complete their work before Christmas vacation. A team member contacted State Senator John Vinich, who visited the school to help with the writing of a formal resolution; he shared two resolutions he had authored for the Wyoming State Legislature.

A former high school science teacher demonstrated the meanings of "resolution" in physics. He explained the resolution of forces to show how an object remains in orbit, and also how resolution describes a lens, which the team later saw applied in astronomy. After discovering the date of the Geminids meteor shower, December 13, the team planned a sleep-over at a home in the country away from the light-polluted sky. Before they finalized their plans, they visited the Weather Bureau for information on sky conditions for that date. The group had a tour of the bureau, including the facility for launching weather balloons. One of the team fathers shared his knowledge about meteors and asteroids while serving as chaperone for the sleep-over. The owner of a camera shop offered advice on night photography and donated the film.

Another kind of "resolution" was demonstrated in music class. The resolution of a chord was shown with recorders: one team member held a G, while another student moved from A to B.

A team member experienced with rocketry suggested they build and launch individual rockets and compute the apogee of flight. Each student made a sextant of a protractor, drinking straw, string, and nut, which proved accurate when compared with the sighting taken on the weather balloon.

The team felt the rocket launch would be an appropriate activity to share with the WSTS residents. They called Joyce Jansa, recreational therapist at WSTS and the mayor of Lander, to invite her "kids" to their launch. At a visit to their school, she introduced her "kids" with a slide presentation of a Special Olympics competition and holiday activities on their grounds. She accepted the invitation to their launch and insisted on a reciprocal visit. When they showed the mayor their resolution, she made plans to read it at a City Council meeting. December 13 was the date chosen so the team could attend before their sleep-over.

December 16 was chosen for the rocket launch because it was predicted to be clear and calm. The art teacher, supervisor of building the rockets, was in charge of the launch pad. During the firing, the group sighted with their sextants and recorded the angles of the apogees as prompted by the school principal. These sightings were used to plot the angle of flight on graph paper. The climax of the afternoon was the launch of the Space Shuttle model *Resolution*.

Following the launch, the children from WSTS were given paper models of a Shuttle that the team had made for them. Mayor Jansa presented the official copy of the resolution that she had read at the council meeting.

Model for the Future

Each student kept a personal log with snapshots of the activities, which were also recorded on videotape. A script was prepared to accompany the tape, which was made available to teachers in the school district and to the WSTS. Both tape and script will serve as models for other classes when they undertake similar projects. The classes will also benefit from the information included.

Bibliography

In addition to the *Readers' Guide to Periodical Literature*, standard encyclopedias and dictionaries, biographies, and general histories, several teams listed the following books as helpful in researching their names and formulating their projects.

Angelucci, Enzo and Attilio Cucari, *Ships*. New York: Greenwich House, 1983.

Armstrong, Richard, *A History of Seafaring, Volume II: The Discoverers*. New York: Praeger Publishers, 1969.

Asimov, Isaac, *Library of the Universe* (The Series). Milwaukee: Gareth Stevens, 1988.

Baker, David, *Today's World in Space* (The Series). Vero Beach, FL: Rourke Enterprises, 1988.

Berger, Josef, *Discoverers of the New World*. New York: American Heritage Publishing Company, 1960.

Blumberg, Rhoda, *Commodore Perry in the Land of the Shogun*. New York: Lothrop, Lee & Shepard Books, 1985.

Blumberg, Rhoda, *The Incredible Journey of Lewis and Clark*. New York: Lothrop, Lee & Shepard Books, 1987.

Bonestell, Chesley, *Rocket to the Moon*. Chicago: Children's Press, 1968.

Branley, Franklyn M., *A Book of Outer Space for You*. New York: Crowell, 1970.

Briggs, Peter, *Water: The Vital Essence*. New York: Harper & Row, 1967.

Brindage, Ruth, *Sailing the Seven Seas*. New York: E.M. Hale and Company, 1962.

Chester, Michael, *Let's Go on a Space Shuttle*. New York: Putnam, 1975.

Clarke, Arthur C., *Life Science Library, Man and Space*. New York: Time-Life Books, 1968.

Colby, C. B., The Colby Books (The Series). New York: Coward-McCann, 1970.

Coombs, Charles, *Passage to Space*. New York: William Morrow & Company, 1979.

Delpar, Helen, ed., *The Discoverers: An Encyclopedia of Exploration*. New York: McGraw-Hill, 1980.

DePauw, Linda Grant, *Seafaring Women*. Boston: Houghton Mifflin, 1982.

Farmer, Gene and Dora J. Hamblin, *First on the Moon*. Boston: Little, Brown & Company, 1970.

Fields, Alice, *Satellites*. New York: F. Watts, 1981.

Forte, Imogene and Joy MacKenzie, *Skillstuff*. Nashville, TN: Incentive Publications Inc., 1980.

Forte, Imogene, Mary Ann Pangle, and Robbie Tupa, *Pumpkins, Pinwheels and Peppermint Packages*. Nashville, TN: Incentive Publications, Inc., 1974.

Fradin, Dennis B., *Explorers*. Chicago: Children's Press, 1984.

Fritz, Jean, *Brendan the Navigator*. New York: Putnam, 1979.

Fritz, Jean, *Where Do You Think You're Going, Christopher Columbus?* New York: Putman, 1980.

Gibson, Michael, *The Vikings*. London: Macdonald Educational, 1976.

Golovnin, V. G., *Around the World on Kamchatka*. Honolulu: Hawaiian Historical Society, 1979.

Grant, Neil, *Explorers*. Morristown, NJ: Silver Burdett Company, 1982.

Grosseck, Joyce and Elizabeth Attwood, *Great Explorers*. Grand Rapids, MI: Gateway Press, 1988.

Hale, John R., *Age of Exploration*. New York: Time, Inc., 1966.

Haws, Duncan, *Ships and the Sea*. London: Hart-Davis, MacGibbon, 1976.

Hicks, Jim, ed., *The Explorers*. Chicago: Time-Life Books, 1984.

Hyde, Margaret O., *Off Into Space*. New York: McGraw-Hill, 1969.

Irvine, Matt, *Satellites and Computers*. New York: F. Watts, 1984.

Landstrom, Bjorn, *The Ship: An Illustrated History*. Garden City, NY: Doubleday, 1983.

Mackie, Dan, *Space Tour*. Milwaukee: Penworthy Publishing Company, 1986.

Marshall, Peter and David Manuel, *From Sea to Shining Sea*. Old Tappan, NJ: Fleming H. Revell Company, 1986.

Maurer, Richard, *The NOVA Space Explorer's Guide: Where to Go and What to See*. New York: Clarkson N. Potter, 1990.

McCall, Edith, *Pioneers on Early Waterways*. Chicago: Children's Press, 1980.

McCall, Edith, *Settlers on a Strange Shore*. Chicago: Children's Press, 1965.

McGowen, Tom, *Album of Spaceflight*. New York: Checkerboard Press, 1987.

Meredith, Robert and Brooks E. Smith, *Exploring the Great River*. Boston: Little, Brown & Company, 1969.

Moche, Dinah L., *The Astronauts*. New York: Random House, 1978.

Morison, Samuel Eliot, *The Great Explorers: The European Discovery of America*. New York: Oxford University Press, 1971.

O'Leary, Brian, *Project Space Station*. Harrisburg, PA: Stackpole Books, 1983.

Oliver, Carl R., *Plane Talk:* Aviators' and Astronauts' Own Stories. Boston: Houghton Mifflin, 1980.

Podendorf, Illa, *True Book of Space*. Chicago: Children's Press, 1982.

Rutland, Johnathan, *All Color World of Ships*. London, WI: Octopus Books Limited, 1978.

Sandak, Cass R., *Explorers and Discovery*. New York: F. Watts, 1983.

Tanner, Fran Averett, *Creative Communication*. Pocatella, ID: Clark Publishing Company, 1985.

Villiers, Captain Alan, *Men, Ships and the Sea*. Washington, DC: The National Geographic Society, 1973.

Von Braun, Wernher and Frederick I. Ordway III, *Space Travel: A History*. New York: Harper & Row Publishers, 1985.

Wayran, Joe, *The Other Side of Reading*. Hamilton, IL: Hamilton Press, Inc., 1980.

Weller, George, *The Story of Submarines*. New York: Random House, 1962.

Zim, Herbert S. and Robert H. Baker, *Stars*. Racine, WI: Western Publishing Company, Inc., 1985.

DIVISION 2

Grades 7–12

Endeavour

Capt. James Cook
of the Endeavour.

Captain James Cook *by William Hodges. This recently discovered portrait of Captain Cook is one of the few pictures of the explorer to be painted from life. Hodges was the official artist on Cook's second voyage to the Pacific, and the picture was probably painted soon after his return to England in July 1775. Courtesy of National Maritime Museum, Greenwich, London.*

Why *Endeavour*

TALLULAH FALLS
SCHOOL, INC.
Tallulah Falls School Road
Tallulah Falls, Georgia 30573

NATIONAL WINNER

Martha K. Cantrell
Team Coordinator
Mathematics Teacher
Grades 8-12

TEAM MEMBERS

Todd Besier (12)
Martha Chan (12)
May Chan (12)
David Farris (10)
Tanya Favus (11)
Kerri Hirsch (11)
Ricky Kuhr (8)
Lee Markham (11)
Damon Wood (10)

The *Endeavour* was the first ship commanded by James Cook, the 18th-century British explorer who did more for defining the map of the world than any explorer before his time. Cook had the same reasons for exploring the Pacific as NASA has for exploring space. He wanted to expand man's knowledge of areas known to exist and of unexplored regions. He increased man's view of earth as NASA's research and exploration have increased man's view of space.

Captain Cook made three very significant voyages. His voyages included the study of geography, hydrography, ethnography, zoology, and botany. He was the first explorer to give scientists prominent roles on his voyages, and therefore, set an important precedent for voyages to follow.

In 1768, British astronomers wanted to make an observation of the transit of Venus which was due in June of 1769. Cook was given command of *Endeavour* to carry out this special mission. In August 1768, *Endeavour* left Plymouth, England, and sailed to the southern hemisphere to make a station at Tahiti. A careful and accurate observation of the transit of Venus would allow the astronomers to determine the distance of the sun from the earth. This distance could then be used as a unit of measurement that would be essential in calculating the parameters of the universe. On June 3, 1769, Cook completed this phase of his mission. The voyage continued around the globe as Cook and his crew explored New Zealand, Australia, and the Great Barrier Reef, where Cook almost lost the *Endeavour* as she ran aground. The flat bottom of the ship prevented her from being torn apart by the coral. "A better ship for such a service I would never wish for," commented Cook of the *Endeavour*. She was a small vessel, only 106 feet long and 20 feet wide. The craft had a round bluff bow which, along with the flat bottom, provided uncommon spaciousness. Cook volunteered the Great Cabin to the naturalists on the expedition. *Endeavour* ended her career in 1795 on a reef along Rhode Island.

Cook's voyage on the *Endeavour* had profound influence on medical theories and science, as well as history. Joseph Banks and Carl Solander, who accompanied Cook on his voyage, became the first naturalists to examine plants and animals in an organized manner around Tierra del Fuego. They collected specimens from more than 100 new plant families with 800 to 1000 new species. They also encountered hundreds of new species of animals. These two men influenced others in the scientific field to explore the Pacific Basin.

[Cook] made his crew follow a strict diet that included cress, sauerkraut, and an orange extract. The voyage of *Endeavour* was the first long-distance voyage on which no man died from scurvy.

Cook's accomplishments aboard the *Endeavour* have inspired men across the years. The Apollo 15 astronauts named their command spacecraft after

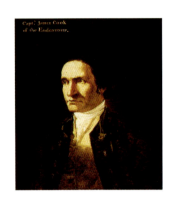

Capt. James Cook
of the Endeavour.

her. The emphasis of the space shuttle program on scientific discovery captures the spirit with which Cook explored new lands and overcame hardships on the *Endeavour* over 200 years ago.

"Endeavour" means to strive for or make an effort to accomplish a project. This exemplifies the spirit of the space program as the steps of accomplishment and advancement in space technology have been taken. From the first walk on the moon in 1969 to the first shuttle launch in 1981, goals have been set and achieved. The word Endeavour directly expresses the reason why our first seven astronauts on the Mercury Project risked their lives to venture into a dangerous, new frontier. They explored the unknown to prove that space exploration was possible.

We believe that the name *Endeavour* captures the spirit of moving ahead and beyond by continuing to set high goals and following the steps necessary to insure the achievement of these goals as NASA continues the flame that Cook lighted by striving for the best in himself, not only for his own country, but for all of mankind.

Math Exploration with James Cook and Where On Earth?. . .

The project chosen by the team was twofold. One part was to emphasize the historical significance of James Cook's voyages, with special emphasis on *Endeavour's* voyage, and the second part was to compare sea exploration to space exploration. The nine-member Tallulah Falls School orbiter-naming team was divided into three groups of equal size after the name *Endeavour* was chosen and the basic components of the project were determined. Two of the three-member groups each assumed responsibility for organizing and writing one part of the project. The third three-member team served as the "computer group," using a word processor to store text, edit documents, and troubleshoot.

A math magazine, *Math Exploration with James Cook,* was chosen as a means of providing information about Cook's travels, particularly aboard *Endeavour,* and of emphasizing the importance of his contributions to world and natural-science exploration. Because Cook was responsible for setting a new standard in British hydrographic surveying by combining land-based trigonometrical surveys with small-boat seaward studies, mathematics seemed an appropriate field with which to combine the historical information.

The "magazine group" wrote the math problems on three levels: Elementary (Level I, grades 1-5); Intermediate (Level II, grades 6-8); and Secondary (Level III, grades 9-12). They chose seven activities to include in each magazine and determined the type of historical information and type of math problems to be used in each. To share their extensive research, they provided a reference list with each magazine.

The second part of the project, a play titled *Where On Earth?. . .,* compared

18th-century exploration on the sea to 20th-century exploration in space, as James Cook and his astronomer, Charles Greene, traveled forward in time from the ship *Endeavour* to the orbiter *Endeavour*. Through the characters' dialogue (the team researched the speech patterns of Cook's time), comparisons were made and information given about both types of travel. The authors showed both similarities and differences.

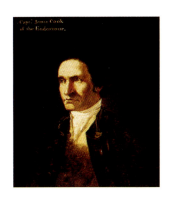

The members of the "play group" determined the sequence of events and how Cook and Greene would travel in time. Each of the three members wrote a portion of the play, and the team coordinator assisted in correlating the three parts. The "play group" also provided a reference list with their finished work.

Model for the Future

The team felt that both the math magazine and the play provide excellent models for future classroom projects and activities. Either can be adapted to many levels and areas of instruction. Both provide a new way to study historical facts that had significant impact on the present.

Within the three levels, the difficulty of the math problems covers a broad range across the mathematics curriculum. The problems can be adapted easily by teachers to fit a particular skill level. The historical information provided should be applicable at any level; only the problems would need to be changed. The magazine also can serve as a model for teachers and students of other subjects in developing a magazine for their own classes.

The play is applicable to a secondary-level world culture class to develop an awareness of the interaction of geography, history, culture, and current events. Middle-school students can perform the play as part of a social studies curriculum. Drama classes can use the script as a skit to introduce several topics such as comparing cultures, exploration in the 18th and 20th centuries, or scientific discoveries made in two different centuries.

Hōkūle'a

Hōkūle'a *sailing off*
Moloka'i Island, 1987.
Photo by Michael A. Tongg,
Honolulu.
Courtesy of Michael A. Tongg.

Why *Hōkūle'a*

The name *Hōkūle'a* (Hoh koo lay-'ah) is appropriate for a space shuttle because it is the name of a sixty-two foot double-hulled anthropological research vessel that began its voyages in 1976. A series of trips throughout the Pacific took the *Hōkūle'a* and its Polynesian crew on a journey of exploration and rediscovery.

Over three thousand years ago Polynesians began making voyages exploring the ocean frontier. The *Hōkūle'a* expeditions provided evidence that early Polynesians discovered new lands and were able to navigate their canoes by using the sun, stars, planets, moon currents, and perhaps most importantly, that they possessed the skills to sail against the prevailing wind.

There are a number of reasons why this name is appropriate for a spacecraft. The name *Hōkūle'a* is Hawaiian, which is a native American language. Although the name may at first appear strange to speakers of English, it is no more difficult to pronounce than Hawaii, and will inspire a sense of wonder. It translates beautifully into English as "The Star of Joy." *Hōkūle'a* is the Hawaiian name for the star we know as Arcturus of the constellation Bootes. It is visible in the sky above the Hawaiian Islands and has been described by the ancient Polynesians as a "homing beacon." The voyage of the *Hōkūle'a* is emblematic of the spirit of exploration. The ancient Polynesians ventured forth into the frontiers of the ocean just as America's astronauts venture forth into the frontiers of space today. Both forms of exploration demonstrate admirable courage, skill, scientific knowledge, and an urge to extend one's horizon to the greatest possible limit.

The ancient Polynesians were regarded by many as the greatest navigators of all time. By naming the Space Shuttle *Hōkūle'a*, Americans will be reminded that many Polynesians have also become Americans. American Samoa is part of the United States and the *Hōkūle'a* expedition proved that Polynesian explorers sailed vast distances to settle what is now the state of Hawaii. We would like the name, *Hōkūle'a*, to serve as Polynesia's connection to America's space program.

The name *Hōkūle'a* would also serve to commemorate Hawaii's first astronaut, Ellison Onizuka, who died in the *Challenger* tragedy. Therefore, we proudly propose the Hawaiian name *Hōkūle'a* for OV 105.

Rediscovering the Polynesian Heritage

The Tafuna High School team's project centered on the construction of a four-foot model of an ancient Samoan seagoing vessel. Their project was important to them because, as Samoa modernizes, it loses contact with the customs, skills, and history that make it what it is today. The actual *Hōkūle'a* was built of fiberglass, but the students built their model in the authentic tradition, using hollowed out

TAFUNA HIGH SCHOOL
c/o Department of Education
Pago Pago,
American Samoa 96799

Paul E. Cassens
Team Coordinator
Chairman, Science
Department

TEAM MEMBERS
GRADES 10-12

Ava'avau Ainu'u (11)
April Buder (11)
Van Cagahastian (10)
Nancy Eli (10)
Puava Moeaiseu (11)
Felicia Moliga (11)
Pine Pine (10)
Filipo Tana'i (10)
Agnes Taylor (11)
Misi Tuumalo (12)
Lealofi Tuna (11)

logs for hulls and woven mats for sails, and planned to stage a mock launching ceremony upon completion of the craft. The *Hōkūle'a* project involved effort from many teachers and students at Tafuna High School, as well as members of the community.

At the time of writing their entry packet, construction of the model had barely begun, but they hoped to have it completed by the end of January 1989. They believed that they would have completed the project by the end of December, but in American Samoa, they tend to receive information about stateside contests at least a month or two later than mainland schools.

Faleomavaega Eni Hunkin, the Lieutenant Governor of American Samoa, who was on one of the *Hōkūle'a* expeditions, lectured at the high school and provided an insight into life aboard such a primitive craft. The J.P. Hayden Museum of American Samoa sent women to teach the students how to weave mats for sails and, under the Artist in Residence program, sent the master carver to teach them how to hollow out logs for the hulls and assist in other aspects of constructing a model of an ancient voyaging canoe. People from the community, parents, Matai (chief) title holders, and the lieutenant governor also assisted them with information about selecting a crew, division of work among the village people as the vessels were constructed, equipping the vessels with provisions for use during the voyage and for establishing a colony on a new island, and departure ceremonies.

The library at the American Samoa Community College permitted the use of its South Pacific collection, from which the students obtained information concerning navigational techniques, village life, and most important, diagrams necessary for the construction of the model.

Students also viewed the videotape entitled *The Navigators* to learn of traditional navigational techniques still being passed along in remote Pacific islands. A speaker from the Land Grant Office, Department of Agriculture, was asked to discuss plants that might be selected to carry on board a voyage for later cultivation in a new land. A medicinal plant collection was started as part of a display when the project would be completed. For this collection, Samoan elders as well as the Director of Health Services, who has a personal interest in medicinal plants of Samoa, were contacted. The students were to receive instruction in the techniques of sailing and, in particular, the skill of sailing into prevailing winds. The project was to culminate with an actual traditional ceremony complete with authentic costumes, presentation of canoe, and traditional protocol. Arrangements would be made with the local television station for coverage of this event.

The learning goals for the project included a rediscovery of the heritage and pride of what Captain Cook called "the Most Extensive Nation on Earth." They also would experience the thrills of anticipation that their ancestors must have felt as they prepared to voyage into the ocean frontier.

Important as traditions, history, and myths may be, the team felt they should not become stagnant ends in themselves. A goal of their project was to transfer the same spirit of discovery that inspired those past explorations to the future—the exploration of space.

Model for the Future

When the model was completed, the team intended to donate it to the museum for public display. An ongoing aspect of the project is a program in which a group of trained students will take the model of the voyaging canoe, along with authentic costumes, to elementary schools on the island. Presentations will include Samoan history of navigating and colonizing of the far-flung Pacific islands.

Endeavour

2-foot Gregorian reflecting telescope, 1763. The Royal Society provided Transit-of-Venus observers with similar telescopes in order to obtain uniform results. This one was made by James Short of London. Courtesy of National Maritime Museum, Greenwich, London.

Why *Endeavour*

*PARKVIEW ARTS
MAGNET SCHOOL
2501 Barrow Road
Little Rock, Arkansas 72204*

*M. Beth Greenway
Team Coordinator
English Instructor
Grade 12*

TEAM MEMBERS

*Jennifer Horton
Matt Hubbard
Brian Skinner
David Ward*

Mankind has always striven to make dreams become reality through exploration, and this fact has never been more appropriately demonstrated than in America's mission in space. Because James Cook's voyage of 1768 was one of great exploratory achievement, it is fitting that his sea vessel the *Endeavour* should serve as the namesake of the NASA Orbiter OV 105. It is also fitting that all exploratory efforts should be lauded; thus, the name *Endeavour* is appropriate because the word itself expresses the desire of humanity to strive for the betterment of society and manifests the idea that one can achieve the impossible by perseverance and determination. In fact, every innovative creation and discovery throughout history could be labeled an endeavor.

Many of Captain Cook's achievements serve as evidence why the name *Endeavour* is appropriate for a spacecraft. Some of these achievements are Cook's discovery of Australia and the Great Barrier Reef and his unprecedented charting of the Pacific. Other outstanding accomplishments on his three year voyage include scientific research, such as the recording of the transit of Venus across the sun and the classification of unknown plant and animal life. These were some of the most important scientific discoveries of his time and helped to pave the way for the future of scientific research and exploration. These examples are the types of achievements that can be accomplished through a spacecraft such as the *Endeavour*.

Since America's mission in space is to expand our world beyond Earth's orbit and to advance our scientific knowledge, the spirit with which James Cook strove to discover unknown realms around the world and the perseverance with which he led his mission can be directly related to the spirit of our mission in space. At the time of Cook's voyage, the only known point in the Pacific was the island of Tahiti. Using this location as his only point of reference, he not only discovered unknown territories, but also managed to chart them so as to create a foundation upon which future exploratory missions could be based. The *Endeavour* voyage was also concerned with collecting and recording scientific data. Similarly, NASA's exploratory mission in space is coupled with scientific research and discovery to help further man's knowledge of space and his universe. Both missions also reflect the effective problem-solving abilities of those involved with the voyages who met many challenges, such as providing proper nutrition and sleeping accommodations and navigating and charting unknown territories. Finally, the will to succeed and the spirit to endeavor are reflected in Cook's three year commitment to the challenges of the South Pacific and in NASA's thirty year commitment to the challenges of space.

The Endeavour: *The Voyage Continues*

Lengthy research narrowed the Parkview Arts Magnet team's choices to six names: *Nautilus* was rejected because it reminded some of the well-known exercise equipment; *Phoenix* would carry with it a constant reminder of the *Challenger* tragedy; *Victory* seemed to have a more militaristic or competitive ring than an exploratory one; and *Eagle* had too clear an association with the first Moon landing; *Pioneer* sounded great, but it seemed to indicate a first-time rather than an ongoing effort. Lively and enlightening discussions led to a unaminous vote for the sixth name, *Endeavour.*

The team chose to produce a slide show because that type of program would be the best possible learning experience; it would combine something they knew a lot about with something about which they knew nothing. They had plenty of experience researching topics—and would need a lot of careful research to write a script for the program—but they knew nothing about the technical aspects of creating a slide show.

The slide show developed into a desire to produce a video, and most team members agreed that a video would make a more effective program, but they also knew that in making a video they would be too dependent upon others and the availability of the studio. Ultimately, they decided to make a slide show, and then, if they had time, they would take their slides to the studio and have them put on tape, substituting video clips for some of the slides.

The Endeavour: *The Voyage Continues* is a space-oriented video. The goals included: (1) To gain a better understanding of space exploration—how it relates to the future of the country and to each person individually; (2) To initiate research relating to two great "golden ages" of exploration—NASA's efforts in the 20th century and Cook's in the 18th—or any great accomplishments in other fields of endeavor; (3) To provide opportunities for creative and divergent thinking through involvement with challenging assignments and projects relating to exploration, research, and discovery; (4) To communicate information clearly, concisely, and effectively through various modes, including written compositions, technical productions, and artistic creations or models.

After students view the presentation, they should be able to:

- Research a famous event or person mentioned in the video or an event or person associated with an exploratory, research, or discovery effort, and design a creative project or write an imaginative composition that clearly demonstrates his or her understanding of the topic.

- Explore, through research, ideas about space and space travel and design a creative project or write an imaginative composition that clearly demonstrates understanding of some aspect of space or space travel or the relationships between space exploration and a particular subject area.

- Complete a research paper that discusses the impact of space on his or her chosen career. As part of the requirements of the paper, the student will write to both a professional in the selected career and a NASA center requesting information relating to the topic.

- Explore, through research, ideas about the future, and design a creative project or write an imaginative composition that effectively demonstrates understanding of the impact that space will have on life in the 21st century.

- Imagine and then solve a problem associated with sea or space travel by designing a creative project that sufficiently demonstrates understanding of a specific problem related to these two modes of travel.

- Read a literary work that reflects an exploratory, research, or discovery endeavor, and design a creative project or write an imaginative composition that effectively demonstrates understanding and/or analysis of the content of the selection.

Model for the Future

This project, coupled with a Teacher's Guide prepared by the team, was designed to be integrated into classes across the curriculum. The general curriculum objectives stated in the guide were written to encompass all the disciplines and academic abilities within a classroom, as well as to provide for maximum teacher flexibility in adapting the video for individual classroom use. Specific assignments and activities were included to suggest the types of projects that would enhance student learning and performance.

Nautilus

*View of the launching of the
USS Nautilus (SSN 571) at
the Electric Boat Co.,
Groton, Connecticut,
January 21, 1954. OFFICIAL
U. S. NAVY PHOTOGRAPH.*

Why *Nautilus*

*BETSY ROSS ARTS
MAGNET SCHOOL
185 Barnes Avenue
New Haven,
Connecticut 06513*

*Robert W. Mellette
Team Coordinator
Chairperson
Science Department
Grades 5-8*

TEAM MEMBERS

*Cuong Bonh (5)
Elizabeth Days (7)
Chris Fairman-Moro (8)
Laura Ginty (7)
Sarah Kaiser (6)
Tim Lavenbein (8)
Nabis Meghelli (6)
Spring Robinson (7)
Hebron Simckes-Joffe (7)
Diallo Stevens (8)
Erika Williams (7)
Tamara Williams (7)*

The Chambered Nautilus is a mollusk found in the deep waters of the South Pacific. Its name is derived from the Greek word for "sailor." As the Nautilus grows, it builds a beautiful chambered spiral shell. A wirelike tube called the siphuncle runs through the middle of the shell connecting each successive chamber of the spiral. According to one theory the siphuncle enables the animal to control the gas pressure of the empty chambers affecting the buoyancy of the shell. This allows the animal to rise to the surface or to sink beneath the waves when faced with danger.

It was this beauty of form and function that possibly inspired Jules Verne to name his fictional submarine the *Nautilus* in his epic adventure *Twenty Thousand Leagues Under the Sea*. In this masterpiece, Jules Verne describes in plausible detail scientific and technological wonders that would not become real for decades after they were described. Jules Verne did not confine his heroes to the marine environment. In some ninety books his heroes travel in spaceships to the Moon, travel *Around the World in Eighty Days,* and even travel to the center of Earth!

Jules Verne's significant contribution to science was that he sowed seeds in the form of ideas that would be harvested by a new breed of more practical dreamers. One of these dreamers was twelve year old Simon Lake. Lake was so impressed by Jules Verne's *Twenty Thousand Leagues Under the Sea,* that after reading it he vowed that one day he would build a submarine like Captain Nemo's *Nautilus*. Thirty years later, Simon Lake fulfilled his ambition. He constructed the first submarine using a double hull like Jules Verne described. His design served as the model for all larger submarines that followed.

On August 3, 1958 science <u>fiction</u> became science <u>fact</u>. An American submarine, the USS *Nautilus* 571 accomplished the "impossible," the first crossing of the geographic North Pole by a sea vessel.

The world's first nuclear powered submarine was the epitome of the shipbuilder's art. The USS *Nautilus* cruised deeper, traveled faster, farther, and longer than any other submarine in history. On its top secret mission to the North Pole, this submarine named after Jules Verne's *Nautilus,* carried an original copy of the book *Twenty Thousand Leagues Under the Sea*.

In honor of this prophetic writer, the state of Connecticut in which the USS *Nautilus* was constructed, and the crewmembers of the *Challenger* spacecraft, we propose the new orbiter OV-105 be christened the *Nautilus*. We feel this is indeed an appropriate name. It is easy to pronounce for radio transmission, it is certainly named after a sea vessel that engaged in research and exploration. The *Nautilus* shattered all previous records for endurance, speed, and distance. It traveled where "no man had gone before," into the unknown and uncharted waters of the last frontier left on Earth. This highly dangerous mission captured the imagination and interest of America.

The skill, professional competence, and courage of the officers and crew of the *Nautilus* was in keeping with the highest tradition of the United States of America and the pioneering spirit that has always characterized our country.

America has always led the world in the peaceful use of technology. The USS *Nautilus* never fired a shot in anger. This ship no longer plies the oceans of the world, but her mission is not complete. Today her mission is EDUCATION. Permanently docked at her pier in Groton, Connecticut, this proud ship and the Submarine Force Library and Museum help the public trace the development and history of the submarine from David Bushnell's *Turtle* to the modern submarines in use today.

John F. Kennedy once said that "space is the new ocean, and we must sail on it." We sincerely hope that the *Nautilus* will someday sail this infinite frontier.

The *Nautilus* Project

The Betsy Ross Arts Magnet School has a full arts curriculum with instruction in visual arts, dance, music, and theatre. Academic instruction includes the traditional program as well as a course in Humanities. After the name *Nautilus* was selected by a Young Astronaut group, because of increased interest by both students and staff, the eighth-grade division was targeted for a multidisciplinary exercise involving the history and development of submarines and an intensive study of the world described by Jules Verne in *Twenty Thousand Leagues Under the Sea*. The school purchased enough paperback copies of the novel for the entire class and it became the textbook for the duration of the project.

In social studies, students read selected passages from the text to find clues that would allow them to chart and plot the voyage of Captain Nemo's *Nautilus*.

In science they traced the history and development of the submarine from Connecticut native David Bushnell's *Turtle* to modern submarines focusing on the similarities between a submarine and the Space Shuttle: both operate in environments that are potentially inhospitable; in both the depressurization of the cabin would be disastrous; all requirements for life must be furnished by the vehicle and monitored constantly; and waste must be managed and controlled. On a field trip to the *Nautilus* at Groton, Connecticut, and from a guest speaker who was actually on the USS *Nautilus* 571 when it went to the North Pole, the class learned that submarines, like the Space Shuttle, have CO_2 scrubbers that remove the buildup of exhaled air. Cabin temperatures are maintained at a comfortable 70°F. During a mission crewmembers must jog in place to maintain fitness. They also learned that with both there is no wasted space—there is room for the crew, but no room for error! Sophisticated navigation systems guide both. In fact, the navigation system used to guide the USS *Nautilus* 571 to the North Pole came from a guided missile.

While learning the scientific aspects of Jules Verne's work in science, students were on a voyage of exploration in art classes. An interdisciplinary team of artists from the visual arts, music, and theatre met with them in a series of intensive workshops designed to raise their awareness of the sights, sounds, and feelings evoked from reading their "textbook." In art, they created collages and montages that expressed their feelings and in music, created and recorded "water sounds."

For the culminating activity in the school library, the class presented a theatre piece using a Geraldo Rivera format (later changed to Al Tersi of Channel 8). After deciding who to interview, what to ask, and the answers, the students took turns being reporters, then crewmen to learn both skills involved. They felt fortunate to have the help and participation of a classmate's parent and the support of many local and community resources. To prepare an appropriate seafood meal, Stop and Shop Supermarket Company donated expensive seafood items. The Yale Peabody Museum of Natural History and the New Haven Historical Society were used for research and information. In January 1989, the New Haven Police S.C.U.B. team planned to demonstrate and explain their equipment.

In true NASA tradition, the Project Nautilus Committee developed an acronym for NAUTILUS - **N**urturing **A**wareness and **U**nderstanding **T**hrough **I**nterdisciplinary **L**earning **U**sing **S**pace.

The majority of time was spent on the preparation of the final production which was staged in the school library so that they could create a more intimate environment. On Thursday, December 22, 1988, The *Nautilus* Project presented its culminating activity to a receptive audience. The participants were immersed in a marine environment with the sights, the sounds, and even the taste of Captain Nemo's underwater world.

Model for the Future

It was not possible to measure the enthusiasm for learning and teaching that the project generated. It had a tremendous educational impact on all who participated and marked not the end, but the beginning of a rich and challenging curriculum that will become part of the school's program.

Horizon

Horizon. *Courtesy of
Scripps Institution of
Oceanography, University
of California—San Diego,
La Jolla, California.*

Why *Horizon*

*JENIFER JUNIOR
HIGH SCHOOL
1213 16th Street
Lewiston, Idaho 83501*

*Steven D. Branting
Team Coordinator
Consultant, Gifted Education
and Special Projects
Grades 6-9*

*TEAM MEMBERS
GRADE 8*

*Teresa Helsley
Clayn Lambert
Alex Pasco
Jenny Ramey
Zach Weenig*

The name *Horizon* was originally used by the Scripps Institute of Oceanography (La Jolla, CA) for a research vessel purchased in 1948 in its marine life research program (Midpac Expedition). The ship had originally been a United States Navy tug, built in 1938. A student won $10 and a drawing of the ship for having supplied the winning entry in a "name-the-ship" contest.

"The *Horizon* was small and not above reproach," said H. William Menard. He added, however: "Few other ships were so honored." As a result of the ship's work, one can find a Horizon Guyot (a submarine plateau or mount) in the central Pacific, a Horizon Depth (second deepest place in the ocean), Horizon Channel near Alaska and Horizon Bank near New Hebrides. During Christmas week of 1952, the *Horizon* dropped a probe near Tonga to a depth of 34,884 feet, then the world's deepest site ever located.

Many of today's leading oceanographers were first trained aboard the *Horizon.* In the twenty years she was used, 132 leading scientists worked under thirteen captains. One of the most famous of these was Roger Revelle. He was the chief scientist on the Midpac Expedition. Noel Ferris and Marv Hopkins were also associated with the ship during various voyages.

The *Horizon* took its last tour in 1967 on what was called the NOVA Expedition to Pago Pago, Samoa; Suva, Fiji; New Caledonia; Auckland, New Zealand; and Brisbane, Australia.

Why would the name *Horizon* be appropriate for America's space program and the OV-105? We submit the following as being important.

1   Both vessels were and are meant for research into man's frontiers. The original *Horizon* was used by leaders in oceanography to complete pioneering experiments. The space shuttle allows physicians, engineers and technicians to do just that in the special world of space.

2   As the *Horizon* was a world leader in oceanographic research and discovery, so the space shuttle has had a similar record in space flight.

3   The word "horizon" itself describes the junction of earth and sky. The space shuttle is a creation of man meant for both. That horizon extends always in front of us no matter where we go, or how fast we are traveling. The word describes a frontier to be gained, but a frontier that always stays one step ahead of us. In his poem "The Wanderer of Liverpool," John Masefield commented: "The skyline is a promise, not a bound."

4   A "horizon" can also describe the range of our perception or understanding. As did the ship *Horizon,* the space shuttle program has already expanded our horizons further than we thought possible.
As R. W. Raymond put it: "A horizon is nothing save the limit of our sight." ("A Commendatory Prayer")

5   *Webster's Third International* (p. 1090) explains that a "horizon" may be "the range . . . of hope and expectation or visible and seemingly attainable end or object." As John Buchan once stated: "Youth . . . demands of life hope and horizon." The future, the "horizon" in space, is a dream of young people today.

6 Additionally, it was the horizon that ancient astronomers used as the tool to set calendars, carefully observing the rising and setting of stars and planets along the line of their farthest sight. Ancient mariners, such as the Polynesians and Chinese, used the horizon to guide themselves from place to place.

Indeed, the name *Horizon* befits a new ship in the United States fleet of space vehicles. The horizons of space are endless. The OV-105 will be one tool to exploring them.

The *Horizon* Project

The team created, organized, and provided learning materials to enrich their school district's classroom instruction concerning America's space program, especially the Space Shuttle. Their objectives produced the following materials:

■ Convergent and divergent thinking: Word searches to familiarize students with space terms; crossword, mazes, and other puzzles about space; videotape listening guides for students; science fair project ideas; space-related simulations and role-playing activities posing hypothetical problems; creative writing activities for individuals and small groups; creative engineering and design activities for classroom and school-wide competitions.

■ History, careers, and spinoffs: Time lines showing historical developments; recommended purchasing lists for school libraries; careers booklet covering aerospace fields; activity for finding space program spinoffs in the home.

■ Space in different subject areas: Creative writing; "Astronaut Training and Fitness Program" for physical education; The Horizon Art Gallery; space travel simulations.

■ Audiovisual materials: Arranged for schools to obtain videotapes through the Teacher Resource Center at the NASA Ames Research Center.

The team packaged the activities in a three-ring binder for teachers, grades 4-9: Black-line duplicating masters for teachers, student handouts, overhead transparency masters, and keys to student sheets. Supplementary learning activities were to be added after evaluation of their project.

In addition, the team planned follow-up activities to:

■ Develop additional materials on request from teachers;

- Update materials based on developments in the space program;

- Have participating schools added to the NASA mailing list.

Model for the Future

The team considered their initial effort as a pilot project to be implemented with participating teachers in February 1989, evaluated by both teachers and students in March, and revised in April. In September 1989, the notebook of materials was to be ready for all district classrooms wishing to use it. They also recommended that future junior high school students be involved in another writing project to update or add to the material produced.

Endeavour

Chart of New Zealand
explored in 1769 and 1770
by Lieutenant J. Cook,
Commander of His
Majesty's Bark *Endeavour.*
*Courtesy of National
Maritime Museum,
Greenwich, London.*

Why *Endeavour*

KIMBALL MIDDLE SCHOOL
451 North McLean Boulevard
Elgin, Illinois 60123

William E. Glennon
Team Coordinator
Earth Science and
Health Education Teacher
Grade 8

TEAM MEMBERS

Emily Burge
Matthew Craker
Dina Rodriguez
Stacy Wolter

The H.M.S. *Endeavour* was a sea vessel which was used both in exploration <u>and</u> in research by Captain James Cook, the famous navigator and explorer who charted a large portion of the Pacific Ocean during his three long voyages. Captain Cook and his crew of sailors and scientists sailed in the *Endeavour* between 1768 and 1771 to explore the southern hemisphere, much of which had not been previously navigated. This expedition also had a scientific research purpose: to observe the planet Venus as it passed between earth and the sun in June of 1769. It was believed that scientists observing this phenomenon, called the transit of Venus, from the ideal position of Tahiti in the South Pacific Ocean would be able to calculate the exact distance between the earth and the sun.

We believe that there is a similarity between the name we are suggesting — *Endeavour* — and the names selected by the National Aeronautics and Space Administration for the other orbiters . . . *Columbia, Challenger, Atlantis,* and *Discovery.* First of all, Webster's Dictionary states that each of the names previously selected by NASA is derived from old English terms, as is "endeavour." There is also an interesting pattern between the three words "challenger," "discovery," and "endeavour" since the letter "c" precedes the letters "d" and "e" just as the orbiter *Challenger* was built and flown before the orbiter *Discovery.* The *Endeavour* would then be a natural alphabetic progression of this pattern.

There is also an especially interesting inter-relationship between the formal definitions of these three words. *Webster's Third New International Dictionary* defines "challenge" as "something that is to be <u>striven</u> for" and that "endeavour" means "to <u>strive</u> to achieve." It also follows that discovery, which is "the act, process or instance of gaining knowledge" is most likely to be successful if it is made with "a serious, determined effort", which is precisely Webster's definition of "endeavour."

The students found several other interesting parallels between the name they proposed and the U.S. space program.

- Captain Cook's first ship was called the *Mercury,* which is also the name of an earlier NASA space program. Another of Captain Cook's vessels was the *Discovery,* which also happens to be the name of another of the Space Shuttles.

- The H.M.S. *Endeavour* carried scientists (astronomers and biologists) on board, just as the OV 105 will when operational. An American sailor, John Gore, was a member of Captain Cook's crew on the *Endeavour.* American naval personnel would undoubtedly travel on board the OV *Endeavour.*

■ Captain Cook's voyages are also especially significant because he never lost any crew members to the dreaded disease that was so common in his day . . . Scurvy.

■ Captain Cook once said of the *Endeavour:* "In such a vessel an able sea officer will be more venturesome and better enabled to fulfill his instructions." What a fine prediction this was for the H.M.S. *Endeavour . . .* and promises to be for the OV *Endeavour.*

Ozone Alerts from Space

After considering many ideas, the team decided on a project concerned with atmospheric ozone. They believe there can be no project more vital to the world community than one that increases knowledge and awareness of the potentially catastrophic changes that are predicted if Earth's ozone layer continues to be destroyed.

Believing that most people are not sufficiently aware of the seriousness of the problem, the team also believes that the space program is ideally suited to carry out the task of informing the world community because of the publicity space flight receives and the fact that astronauts and other NASA personnel are highly respected and have a high degree of credibility. They believe that NASA should take the initiative in alerting the world community to the nature and the extent of the ozone problem and to be the first to begin to take effective action.

The team's project consists of an educational model referred to as *Ozone Alerts from Space.* Each alert would be composed of three basic parts: (1) Informational—During a space flight telecast the Shuttle crew could explain the ozone layer and the ozone loss; (2) Demonstrational—A telecast could explain and show production of ozone as well as its destruction during the chemical reaction between ozone and chlorofluorocarbons (CFCs); and (3) Experimental—Two phases of experimentation are suggested: one involves intercepting and destroying the chlorofluorocarbons before they reach the ozone layer, and a second involves replenishing the ozone layer either with ozone or an ozone substitute.

The *Ozone Alert from Space* telecasts could be patterned after the Teacher In Space project. Several different presentations could be prepared, with one intended for the general public and others for elementary level students, middle school/ junior high school classes, and senior high school or college students. In this way, each target group would receive the information that is most suitable for them.

As middle school students, the team recognized their lack of the scientific expertise needed to develop their ideas into final form. That would be the task of professional scientists. However, they suggested that the ozone destruction problem could be approached simultaneously in several different ways:

■ Continued production and use of chlorofluorocarbons (CFCs) must be stopped and suitable substitutes found.

■ Substances may be found that can be released into the atmosphere to interrupt and interact with CFCs before they can destroy the ozone. Such substances could be referred to as "CFC deactivators."

■ Methods of producing ozone inexpensively and releasing it into the atmosphere to replace lost ozone should be developed. Ozone might be jettisoned at appropriate altitudes as spacecraft travel through the ozone layer during launch and reentry maneuvers.

The team considers the first logical step to be educating and alerting a large part of Earth's population, and believes that no group has a better opportunity to carry out this important informational first step than NASA. A series of well-prepared presentations telecast from outer space will reach more people and will be better received than any number of well-written stories offered by the conventional media.

Model for the Future

If accepted and implemented by NASA, the team feels their project can influence learning throughout the world, not only in classrooms and schools, but in research laboratories, governmental chambers, and business boardrooms.

If NASA uses their project to alert the world to the ozone crisis and then demonstrates ways to solve the problem, it could be the beginning of a world-wide effort. Not only could other nations begin to take corrective measures here on Earth, but those countries that have their own space programs could join U.S. space efforts in correcting the ozone problem. If such a spirit of worldwide cooperation, concern, and effort should eventually develop, the orbiter vehicle *Endeavour* will have accomplished its mission and will have lived up to the formal definition of endeavour, which is "a conscientious or concerted effort toward a given end."

Desire

Thomas Cavendish.
*Courtesy of National
Portrait Gallery, London.*

Why *Desire*

Boone Grove Junior/
Senior High School
325 West 550 South
Boone Grove, Indiana 46302

David A. Kahn
Team Coordinator
Chemistry and Biology
Teacher, Grades 7-12

TEAM MEMBERS

Joe DeLeon (11)
Kathleen Kosmoski (11)
Andy Maxwell (12)
Jim Mowery (11)
Chris Nehring (12)
Frank Ulburgs (12)

Galileo, Ponce deLeon, Isaac Newton, Thomas Edison, Magellan, these and countless others dreamed, sought after, and found better lives through knowledge of the unknown. Each had the desire and stamina to fulfill their dreams.

Today is no different. More discoveries in medicine, science, and technology have erupted in the past fifty years than in all the years before. We have an insatiable appetite and desire for unravelling the mysteries of the universe.

The great ship *Desire* circled the globe over 400 years ago in an effort to retrace the circumnavigation of Sir Francis Drake of only a few years earlier. Thomas Cavendish piloted the *Desire* back to England in 1586 after losing two other ships on the treacherous voyage from England to Brazil, then down to Argentina. There, he discovered what we know today as Port Desire before continuing through the Strait of Magellan, crossing the mighty Pacific, then sailing home by way of the Philippines and Cape of Good Hope.

A desire to discover the unknown, to find new frontiers, a better life, were paramount to the success of those listed above. Cavendish and the *Desire* built upon earlier discoveries, successes, and knowledge to fulfill their mission. The space shuttle Desire will also build upon and enhance the knowledge gained from her sister shuttles: *Atlantis, Challenger, Columbia,* and *Discovery.*

The word "desire" emphasizes a positive attitude and striving to reach new heights and a maximum potential. This is the same spirit that pervades America's space program and put us in the forefront of space exploration and technology. Without our craving for education and knowledge, our horizons would be limited, inflexible, and ultimately static. No longer could we maintain the prominence and pride we now enjoy because of our desire to learn. Is there a more appropriate name for OV 105 than *Desire*? We think not. Can it be easily heard on the radio? Was it the name of an exploring vessel? Does it capture the spirit? Does it sound "good"? We answer yes to all of these questions. What other name can capture our spirit of space exploration as much as *Desire*? Desire is the embodiment of our mission in space, the embodiment of learning, of succeeding.

Simply stated the word "desire" means a strong longing for. Isn't that what the space program is all about? Desire, the basis for discovering the unknown. Desire, the basis of all learning.

Desire, America's space mission personified, our next Orbiter.

A Learning Disk and a Board Game

The team wanted a project that would be educational for themselves as well as those who use it and that would serve as a resource for teaching at their school.

They developed two games, a computer game and a board game, for grade levels 4-7 and 8-12 that covered six categories.

For the students, the name *Desire* indicated a willingness to learn. The team felt that students have the desire to learn about space exploration and will desire to participate in their learning games. The computer learning kit will help broaden students' frontiers with a new look at the study of space; the board game will help motivate students to research on their own. Both are challenging, competitive, and educational, projects that can be used as an alternative form of teaching for all levels of students.

Desire Learning Disk

The team called the computer learning game they engineered the *Desire* Learning Disk. It contains nearly 700 questions about the space program, including history of space exploration, science in space, mathematical problems of space study, space terminology, arts in space, and astronomy. During play, the computer selects a number at random to be counted down from "T-minus 50" as questions are answered correctly. The first team to reach "T-minus 0" is declared the winner of the learning game by seeing "Lift-Off" printed in red, white, and blue followed by a congratulations for successfully completing their mission. The team wants participants to know the right answers to all questions, and feels the game will motivate students to research topics of space study.

Putting the computer program together (on an Apple IIgs computer) was an effort entailing many hours of writing creative questions, typing them onto the computer, proofreading, and incorporating the questions into the computer learning program.

Desire Learning Board Game

The educational board game the team developed is based on the same principles as the computer game. The board game is played on a felt surface containing a Shuttle and 50 hexagonal spaces. Players challenge each other's knowledge and problem-solving skills by answering questions and try to be the first to reach a point of 0, which is designated "lift-off point."

The *Desire* Learning Board Game uses different colors on the numbered hexagons to represent the several parts of an astronaut's prelaunch schedule. After answering questions correctly to move through each colored hexagon section, players complete the following series of activities:

50 - 44 green	Congratulations. You have been selected for an astronaut training program.
43 - 37 brown	You have been selected for a Shuttle crew position of pilot, mission specialist, or payload specialist.

36 - 31 yellow	Your efforts have enabled you to successfully complete the astronaut fitness training program.
30 - 25 hot pink	A Shuttle flight assignment has been scheduled in the near future.
24 - 19 blue	You will be fitted for a space suit and accessories.
18 - 13 tan	You have just entered the Shuttle and are preparing for launch.
12 - 7 light pink	A final check has been made on all controls. All systems go for launch.
6 - 1 purple	We have ignition.
0 red	Lift-off point.

A major task for the team was printing close to 700 multiple-choice questions on cards, typing answers, laminating the cards, and cutting them to a uniform size.

Parents, students, teachers, and school support staff helped with the organization and production of both parts of the project—especially the school's second year computer-programming class, a science teacher who spent hours working out the "bugs" in the program, media specialists who helped with the game cards, the school secretary, and the team coordinator's wife who sewed the felt game board.

A Model for the Future

Both parts of the team's project include all major fields of study at their school, and enhance the curriculum by covering an area that is not studied on a regular basis—space exploration. Thus, the project serves as a model for future programs in all disciplines. It was donated to the school library with the stipulation that future students will add questions to keep pace with new discoveries and advancements.

Resolution

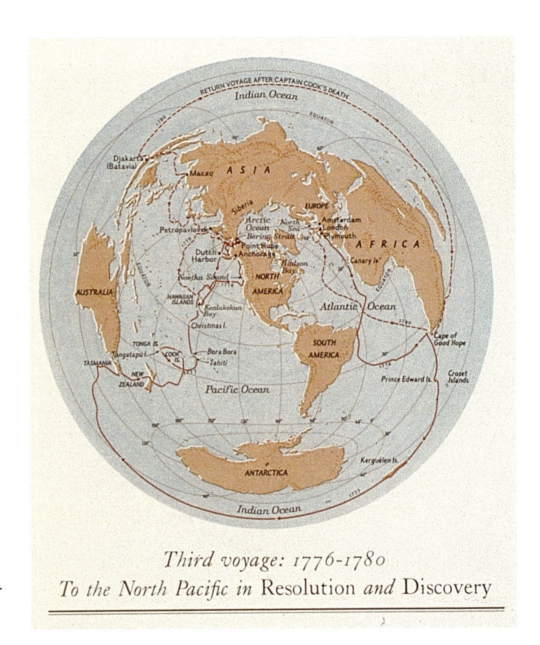

Map of Cook's third voyage. (c) National Geographic Society. Used with permission.

Why *Resolution*

CALDWELL COUNTY
MIDDLE SCHOOL
Princeton, Kentucky 42445

Marlene B. Coursey
Team Coordinator
Science Teacher, Grade 8

TEAM MEMBERS
Christy Littlefield
Chris Martin
John Ramsey
Josh Stasium
Bobby Strong
Anzie Story
Marla Trusty
Len Young

We have chosen the name *Resolution* from an exploring ship under the command of Captain Cook. Her contribution in a variety of areas parallel those soon to be explored by OV-105.

Commanded by James Cook, a proclaimed explorer, the *Resolution* was destined for greatness. The orbiter OV-105 is also destined for greatness. She, too, will be carrying well-trained crews, the best available in today's world, as was the crew of the *Resolution* in her day. The *Resolution* carried out many missions on her exploration voyages including studies by naturalists and astronomers, and OV-105 will also be involved in a variety of missions. Captain Cook tried new inventions, including John Harrison's chronometer No. 4. It was the first time that he had been able to convert time to tell his East-West position. OV-105 will also try new equipment. . . .

Captain Cook searched for a legendary continent populated by many people, and the search for life on other planets continues. Bravery was a way of life for the crew of the *Resolution*. They sailed from areas where it was so cold that icicles hung from their noses, and their clothes were as frozen suits of armor...their hands could scarcely grasp the ropes...sailed on to tropical heat so stifling that not even a breeze was present to ripple a sail or cool their brows. Physical discomfort will be present with the crew of the orbiter, also, but their complaints will not be voiced, for the spirit of adventure will be stronger than anything else.

The *Resolution* continued on her mission when her sister ship returned home in fear due to the untimely and bizarre deaths of some of the crew members. Resolve to continue the space program after the death of the seven crew members of the Challenger shows the same strength. The *Resolution* searched for a passageway between the Pacific and the Atlantic Oceans. The new orbiter will be searching for a passageway from earth to faraway places in space.

We are proud to submit the name *Resolution* for the new orbiter. We believe the loyalty, the bravery, the will to fight against adverse situations and to continue on against all odds, which the *Resolution* and her crew exhibited, is the spirit of the space program today.

A Radio Script and a Lesson Plan

When the orbiter-naming entry packet arrived, excitement was high. The students planned a Space Day; invited the NASA Spacemobile; put up posters; and sent two students, who won an essay contest for the trip, to meet a visiting astronaut and the governor of Kentucky.

Their first problem was research. Armed with the suggested book list, they found the school library had none on the list, the high school library had two, and the public library had only five. Just when they felt the project was grounded, their regional librarian obtained 15 more books from Frankfort, the state capital. They created a special resource room.

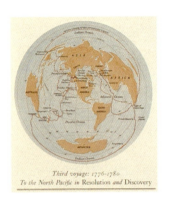

Third voyage: 1776–1780
To the North Pacific in Resolution and Discovery

Where a Student Has Never Been Before

The team began their project with a radio script that explained the orbiter-naming competition and how they, as a team, felt about the space program. To accomplish this, they needed teachers to help edit; the local radio manager for air time; business people to let them put their program on the air; and their parents to support them and get them to the station.

Success was a broadcast, *Where a Student Has Never Been Before,* on December 30, 1988, at 12:30 p.m. After an introduction by the team coordinator, five students discussed the competition and the aftermath of the *Challenger* accident. And how sad they were that their dream of a "Student in Space" following the Teacher in Space, was gone. They had all "had this dream, somewhere, sometime, of walking up that ramp, smiling, waving, so straight in our blue jumpsuits."

Then, a successful flight, and the thrill and pride and tenseness and unity that comes with every ignition and liftoff. And the Orbiter-Naming Program revived their dream of going "where a student has never been before." They would "ride through the shaking fury of a lift-off on the Shuttle . . . glide past the silvery glow of the smiling Moon, . . . could be there on the Shuttle bearing the name we gave it. Our work, our project, our pride in naming the Shuttle would be a dream come true with each majestic flight of the orbiter which would bear the name we had searched so hard to find, the name which personified the feelings of students everywhere, the *Resolution.* Yes, the *Resolution* will truly take us . . . where a student has never been before."

Man's Resolution to Fly

The radio program was a short-term, one-time thing, so the team developed another, long-lasting project. To teach younger students some of the things they had learned while doing their research, they decided to write and present the history of flight to a third grade class. Then, because there were four boys and four girls on the team, they decided to split up and teach two classes.

A fast-approaching deadline welded the team into a solid unit of hard-working, enthusiastic, volunteers-for-all-duties, arranging their schedules to complete their project. Their goal was to go to the third grade; to have an hour with them to soar in imagination to man's earliest dream of flight; to show them the realization of those dreams and to talk about the present; to tell about their project and the name Resolution; and finally, to make the children feel included as part of the team.

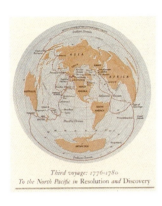

Third voyage: 1776-1780
To the North Pacific in Resolution and Discovery

■ They began with a title, *Man's Resolution to Fly.* In teams of two, they researched man's dream of flying, from first attempts to the present time, when those resolutions have become an open-ended reality. They discovered Daedalus and Icarus in Greek mythology, and decided this would be a good attention-getter for third-graders. Another group found Leonardo da Vinci's design for a flying machine. Then they researched balloons, dirigibles, gliders, the Wright Brothers, planes of all kinds, and finally "the beautiful, powerful, complexity of the Space Shuttles."

■ The next step was preparing a lesson plan. The objectives were to give the students an overview of both the history and the future of flight, to explain why they were visiting the classes, and why they chose the name *Resolution.*

■ In searching for information, they found a "perfect little booklet" in a packet of elementary school materials and were able to outline what they wanted to say. Then they put together their own book for the third-graders with the history of flying, word games, and puzzles with secret messages.

■ They planned to close by talking with them about synonyms, and telling them what they found in the dictionary for resolution, inspiring words that expressed their own feelings about the space program and the OV-105— courage, decision, determination, firmness, fortitude, separation, disentanglement, dissolution, resolvedness, resoluteness, constancy, perseverance, steadfastness, boldness, purpose, resolve—words that portray what OV-105 signifies to students and to Americans of all ages.

With lesson plans, handouts, and all materials prepared, the teams asked for and received permission to visit two classes on January 5, 1989. "Our final step was practicing for that awesome moment when twenty plus pairs of eyes would be staring at us as we stood before them, wanting them to feel the thrill of Kitty Hawk - to remember how we sat almost not breathing watching the last shuttle being launched, and to feel a part of our team, now, as we proudly submitted our name *Resolution.*"

Model for the Future

The lesson plan was designed as a project that could be repeated year after year.

Victory

DEPARTURE OF CAPT. ROSS FROM WOOLWICH ON HIS LAST EXPEDITION MAY 23rd 1829

Illustration from Last Voyage of Capt. Sir John Ross *by Robert Huish. London, 1836. Courtesy of Library of Congress.*

Why *Victory*

OTTOSON JUNIOR
HIGH SCHOOL
63 Acton Street
Arlington, Massachusetts
02174

Marie J. Neal
Team Coordinator
Science Teacher, Grade 7

TEAM MEMBERS

Becky Anderson
Thomas Arria
Jessica Bina
Julie Brusgulis
Allison Burns
Katelyn Caffelle
Aileen Carr
Anthony Fine
Jean Galluccio
Andrea Lionetta
Christine McCall
Alison O'Leary
Matthew Prescott
Olivia Segard
Tasha Sevland
Sean Shanda
Robby Sheahan
Kenneth Shelton
Doug Shen
Deanna Stacchi
Tim Sullivan
Ellen Takata
James Tatosky
Eileen Tighe
Sheila Walden

We propose the name *Victory* to honor the paddle steamer of Captain John Ross and his talented nephew and second-in-command, James Clark Ross. Their steamship *Victory* braved the polar waters in a struggle to uncover a Northwest Passage. Sponsored by Sir Felix Booth, the expedition of the eighty-seven ton *Victory* experienced difficulties due to its steam engine.

A private venture, *Victory's* journey began in 1829, by way of Prince Regent Inlet in the Northwest Territory, Canada, but it was never to reach its destination. Ensuing engine problems and worsening weather conditions finally forced its landfall on the east coast of the Boothia Peninsula, Northwest Territory, where the ship would remain and house its crew for the next three winters.

Time was not wasted, however. The Rosses took advantage of this opportunity to observe the nearby culture and techniques of polar land travel and to study magnetism. On May 31, 1831, using Eskimo methods of transportation, James Clark Ross pinpointed the exact location of the North Magnetic Pole.

Eventually, the *Victory's* crew and captain had to abandon the ship and left it, using various boats to make their final trip to Lancaster Sound, where a British whaling ship rescued the men and returned them to England.

The name *Victory* is appropriate for the OV 105 Shuttle, for it carries a clear and concise message and symbolizes a feeling we all have experienced. It tells of a need to take courage, to conquer and overcome the fears and setbacks of the past. We hope this spacecraft will brighten the shadow and shock brought on by the *Challenger* tragedy, and bring back the enthusiasm, pride, and comfort of once again having successful space travel in America.

The American winning spirit and ambition is captured in the name *Victory,* as it is probably the dream and need of most people to achieve a personal victory of some kind in their lives, no matter how small or large. This must be how the Rosses felt, as they persevered and made an important discovery even after their ship crumbled. As the OV 105 makes history, its name may be kept in the hearts and minds of Americans as an inspiration for future space travel, and hopefully, as a ship that lives up to, and perhaps beyond, its name.

A Quilt

The team submitted a quilt as a symbol of their patriotic interest in the welfare of the United States, and with great enthusiasm pursued their ambition to name the OV-105, *Victory.*

The steps on the quilt show the steps by which the United States gradually achieved victory in becoming a leading figure in worldwide aeronautics. Victory symbolizes the work the United States has done to secure goals of finding new places for resources and residences that will soon be required for the evergrowing population of the world.

Teams were charged with discovering two names to submit to the class. The students met in the school media center to complete the research, using books from the two other secondary schools in Arlington in addition to their own. Each team presented its choice of names to the class and defended its choices in response to questions, challenges, and discussions that followed each presentation. On November 7, the team decided on a method of voting for the one name that would be submitted. On November 8, Election Day for the entire country, the name was selected by a combination of elimination rounds and secret ballot.

The next week, students decided on a format to present the name—a quilt. The quilt, which has a historical tradition unique to the United States, included the disciplines of art, home economics, graphic design, writing, and mathematics in completing the project. Sketches were made, ideas were discussed, and the final design collaboration was completed. Then the students enlarged their sketches and transferred them to fabric in the graphics shop. Oil crayons, indelible markers, and acrylic paints were used to complete the colorful squares. A faculty member, who is an accomplished quiltmaker, sewed the quilt together.

The quilt consists of 25 squares. Each square was made by one student in the class, but everyone cooperated to insure that they would fit together properly. Above the NASA logo, which expresses their national pride in the space program, there is a map of the route that the steamboat *Victory* traveled in 1829 in its attempt to discover a northwest passage. In the center, in a diagonal row, are illustrated what the team thought were the United States' most important victories in space. The first square, at the lower right, shows a picture of the steamboat *Victory* from which the team got their name. The second victory pictured is the Mercury spacecraft, the first program to put Americans in space. The next achievement was the Saturn V launch vehicle, part of the Apollo program, which provided the first vessel to reach the Moon. The next important step in the exploration of space was *Skylab,* which enabled people to remain in space for extended periods of time. The latest victory is the Space Shuttle, a reusable vehicle which will further the possibilities of regular space travel for citizens of the United States.

At the end of the competition, the local paper was to carry a story about the project, and the quilt itself was to be displayed in the administrative offices of the school. In May 1989, a local community arts group of 250 members, the Quilter's Connection, planned to display the quilt in their annual quilt show, where viewers usually number over a thousand. In discussing the final disposition of their creative work, the students' suggestions included a raffle to raise money for a worthy cause, donation to an organization where it would be permanently displayed, and leaving it within the school system.

Model for the Future

Multidisciplinary educational practices are not unusual in gifted and talented programs; however, the team felt that their project serves as an impetus for teachers in the Arlington public school system to appreciate the talents of all students when structuring lessons. In their project, "the work of the artistic students can be seen, and the work of the promising writers can be read, but what is not evident are the results of those students who possess leadership skills and analytical abilities. Students who excel in these areas, and those who have the ability to relate to others, are the quiet movers who establish the rules for group dynamics. Without them, a project such as this would not come to fruition."

Calypso

Calypso. *Courtesy of The
Cousteau Society, member
supported, nonprofit
environmental organization.*

Why *Calypso*

BENILDE-ST. MARGARET'S
HIGH SCHOOL
2501 South Highway 100
St. Louis Park, Minnesota
55416

Mary Jo Aiken
Team Coordinator
Mathematics Teacher
Grades 9-12

TEAM MEMBERS
GRADE 10

Matthew Dooley
Jennifer Murphy
Janine O'Malley
Ryan Palacek
Molly Ryan

We are proposing the name *Calypso* for OV-105.

It is a wonderful name with a deep international history. The ocean research vessel *Calypso* was purchased by the Frenchman Jacques-Yves Cousteau in Malta in the year 1944. The ship was built in the United States in 1942 for the Royal Navy and used as a ferry between Malta and Gozzo. We would like to think that a *Calypso* in space would promote international cooperation, peace, and a shared knowledge of our universe.

Calypso's crew from the very first had a very cohesive personality. They were companions in adventure and education. They were always a team and enjoyed each other. They even had their own Calypso song. The very nature of life on the shuttle suggests a parallel approach would be the only sane one. And why not a little Calypso music? It stirs the rhythm of the soul and the creativity of the heart.

Cousteau himself, while observing his first satellite in the night sky, said "The heavens are not so distant after all, I think to myself! Humans can draw circles of starlight in the night skies just as they do in the night waters." President Kennedy called this sky "the new ocean" of space.

The name also goes back to the classics. On the 11th stop of his return trip home from the Trojan War, Odysseus survived a tempest by swimming to a nearby island inhabited by the goddess Calypso and her nymphs. She was the goddess of beauty and serenity, two attributes so closely associated with space. This is why there is a nymph swimming beside a dolphin on the Calypsonian patch.

The children of the future will be raised with the benefits and spinoffs of space exploration just as we are reaping the benefits and spinoffs of ocean exploration. We have to lose an earthbound vision of ourselves. The world is more than Mother Earth. It is above us, under us, and all around us.

Cousteau has gone farther and deeper exploring the sea than anyone in history and he has used *Calypso* as his home base. Now it's time to go farther and higher in space exploration than anyone ever dreamed using a similar base called *Calypso*. We feel there is a strong parallel between the scientific quest of the sea and the scientific quest of space using all of our technological innovations coupled with our need for personal and collective adventure. Progress only comes from exploration and the success of our predecessors is encouraging.

Jacques-Yves Cousteau took his oceanauts to the depths of the sea on *Calypso* and we would like to see NASA take our astronauts to depths of space on a new and beautiful *Calypso*. The very mention of the name suggests successful exploration to the world. Why not ride it further and higher?

It has a beautiful sound. "Come in, CALYPSO."

Calypso *Too*

The team's project, Calypso *Too*, was designed to stir the enthusiasm of students about the space program. Just as their parents grew up with the excitement of reaching into space for the first time and applauding every new discovery, their own generation has grown up expecting miracles in space. They felt that somewhere teaching has to show that these things are caused and controlled by people. They wanted to communicate that the space program needs more than mathematicians and scientists, that dreams cause things to happen.

In addition to library research, the team asked for suggestions from teachers in other departments, as well as from their families and other students. One English teacher was so excited, he wrote up the basic instructions on limericks and said he would like to use them during national English week. The art department allowed students to work on patch designs. The administration was delighted to see students with an interdisciplinary thrust which is so often lost in high school.

To contribute to education, specifically space education, in their community, the team created several teaching units. Each was introduced with a background of calypso music and a statement that this was "*Calypso* Too!" They wanted their audience to know that "calypso" means many things . . . spontaneity, excitement, emotion . . . that it is music . . . that it has a rich heritage in the Cousteau sea explorations . . . and that it is a wonderful name for a vehicle involved in space exploration.

Their intentions were to reach out and teach different age levels and interest groups by using packets that could be adapted with little difficulty and addressed several disciplines. Contests were held in classes, and small prizes awarded.

- **Limerick:** The English Department contributed the easy rules. A discussion was held in class concerning the nature of limericks, and samples were presented.

- **Patch Design:** Every NASA group has its own patch. Several teachers showed NASA patches and explained the designs, and students were invited to bring in any they had. Jacques Cousteau's *Calypso* patch was discussed, along with an explanation of its Greek affiliation.

- **Lyrics:** Calypso music is a wonderful rhythm, and people react readily to its beat. One of the team members, a gifted young pianist, presented his own variations of familiar songs. Tapes were also played, and teams of 3, 4, and 5 students wrote Shuttle-related lyrics to a tune.

- **Quotations:** This packet was introduced by a discussion of "What does your world look like?" A set of world maps, distorted to fit different geometric solids (Creative Publications), was displayed, followed by strong suggestions that today's world had to contain the sea and land and also space. Quotes were taken from several books on and by Cousteau relating to sea explorations. Students were asked to draw parallels between the sea and space. Many of the quotes could be directly applied to the Shuttle program. This presentation naturally led to a discussion of the use of maps, NASA Spinoff books, and related magazines.

- ■ *Multilingual coloring book:* Simple space-related drawings—Shuttle, astronauts, Space Station, etc.—were duplicated for young children to color. Each picture was labeled in English, Spanish, French, German, and Russian. Each language was represented on the team and students checked the translations with the respective foreign language teacher.

- ■ *Word-search:* Word-search sheets were developed for three different difficulty levels varying from 10 words to 50 words. The more difficult ones also allowed word reversal. They were designed to enhance vocabulary and spelling.

The projects were presented to several groups. The geometry class to which the team belonged served as the major field test group, and each packet was presented on a different day. In addition, one of the community grade schools assisted by testing the word search, limericks, and patch design contest.

Each participating group received an explanation of the program and an enthusiastic message on space exploration from the team members making the presentation.

Model for the Future

The project proved to be adaptable to all ages. Its popularity resulted in requests for teams to continue classroom visits, thus setting the stage for an ongoing program.

Phoenix

Phoenix, 1809, *first class postage stamp. Courtesy of United States Postal Service.*

Why *Phoenix*

HELENA HIGH SCHOOL
1300 Billings Avenue
Helena, Montana 59601

Paul L. Dorrance
Team Coordinator
Physics, Electronics, and
Trigonometry Instructor
Grades 10-12

TEAM MEMBERS

Steve Brackman (12)
Tiffany Freeman (12)
Paul Humphreys (12)
Missy Jaeb (12)
Amanda Slevira (11)
Matt Wilson (12)

The name *Phoenix* was chosen from the first sea going steamship that made its exploratory sea going journey in 1809. The steamship *Phoenix* was used for research by Moses Rogers, when he piloted the "first steamship to go to sea" in 1809 and ushered in a new era of transportation across the oceans. Just as the orbiter *Phoenix* will usher in a new era of transportation across the solar system.

The name *Phoenix* seems to bring with it a bit of luck. The steamship *Phoenix* was hardly seaworthy, had a temperamental engine, and was "nursed" from Hoboken to Philadelphia, taking two weeks to complete the journey.

The name *Phoenix* is appropriate because of its mythological meaning. In Greek mythology the phoenix was a beautiful bird that had a specific life span. After a fiery death, a new phoenix rose from the ashes carrying many of the same characteristics of the deceased phoenix. Like the phoenix, the *Challenger* faced a fiery death, but a new shuttle will replace the *Challenger* and will rise from Space Port USA carrying the hopes of America, as we move toward the next phases of the space program, the Space Station and beyond.

The United States space program has been characterized by adventure, excitement and hope. Moses Rogers personally felt all these emotions during his two week adventure "hugging the coast and nursing fragile paddle wheels and a hull that could hardly be called seaworthy" all the while envisioning steam powered crossings of the Atlantic, which he would accomplish eleven years later. The orbiter *Phoenix* will carry this spirit as each launch into low earth orbit is a prelude to crossings of the solar system.

Lessons for EDUNET (EDUcational NETwork)

Unanimously, excitedly, the team wanted the name Phoenix because to them it symbolized rebirth, but they had difficulty finding the ship. They talked to parents and teachers and searched school, city, and college libraries. No stone was left unturned. Discouragement set in and they feared they would have to abandon the perfect name. However, after so much work they had decided that the rebirth of the phoenix also symbolizes the rebirth of education in today's technological world, so they continued the search.

When they pretty much gave up on Phoenix and tried to think of other names, nothing "fit." Then, the newly-elected chairman of their team came across the bit of information needed in an obscure book in the back of the college library on what he described as the last hour he was going to spend searching for a research vessel named *Phoenix*. He found the *Phoenix* described as the first steam powered ship to be a seagoing vessel. Perseverance had produced the 1809 steamship as the cornerstone for their project. They could continue with their dream.

Phoenix 1809

After many discussions, the team agreed on a set of lessons for students, K-12, in three areas of study, and prepared the lessons to be accessed on the EDUNET system.

For the previous seven years, EDUNET had forged a rebirth of education to remote schools, providing opportunities for students that otherwise would not be available. EDUNET is an individualized, interactive, mastery learning NETWORK that connects teachers and students in a one-on-one learning situation, no matter where they are located—truly an educational system for the 21st century rising from the ashes of the *Nation at Risk* report on education.

The goals of the team's project were to take each of four different grade levels through each of three different subjects—Mythology, Beginning Exploration and Ships, and Space Exploration. The 12 lessons created stressed different skills at different levels:

- The K-3 level emphasized imagination, creativity, and art;

- The 4-6 level expanded to reading, beginning research, and writing skills;

- The 7-10 level added public speaking skills to the previous skills; and

- The 11-12 level emphasized teamwork.

The team split into three mini-teams to write the lessons for the three subject areas, then returned to the original group to create the common parts necessary to complete the lessons: an evaluation form for students, the master list of reference material, and the introduction to the 12 lessons. The lessons were given to teachers at the various grade levels for review and, after incorporating their suggestions, were tested with students at each grade level. The feedback from this process was to be included in the final lessons.

Model for the Future

The lessons can be incorporated into any set of curriculum objectives to whatever depth a teacher or school desires. The team left many options for teachers and students to integrate the lessons into other areas of study, thus providing another way for students to gain the skills necessary to function in a technological world.

The team felt that as education moves into the 21st century, schools will play a different role in society. The Information Age will allow students access to all the knowledge they have, the time and desire to learn via wrist watch, computer, or satellite link to any data base in the world. Education on the Earth-Mars orbiting space platform will be delivered differently than traditional lectures in a classroom. Schools may well become a place for student social interaction, while the information needed to acquire knowledge/skills will be delivered on an individualized, ready-to-learn basis. It will not be necessary to have a lock-step, time-dependent system of education. We will all be students all our lives. Everyone will move as far and as fast as time and abilities allow through an educational system that will be everywhere all the time.

This is a phoenix-like rebirth of education that has its beginnings in a system like EDUNET.

The lessons for this system are available to students anywhere there is a phone line 24 hours a day, 365 days a year on an individualized basis. "The future is here now, what we can dream; can be."

Resolution

Model of Resolution.
Courtesy of Anchorage
Museum of History and
Art, Alaska.

Why *Resolution*

J.H.S. 118X/
WILLIAM W. NILES/
P.A.C.E. ACADEMY
577 East 179th Street
Bronx, New York 10457

Allen L. Kurtz
Team Coordinator
Literature Teacher
Grades 7-9

TEAM MEMBERS
GRADE 8

Lettisha Boyd
Ruby Brooks
Sakina Brown
Melissa Cartagena
Bun Khirt Cheng
Pyong Cho
Yvonne Cruz
Nicole Davis
Manny DeJesus
Jerome Dendy
Francisco Grimaldi
Neil Hosein
Bianca Jackson
Igloris Jerez
Doreen Luckey
Wayne Moffit
Jace Ocasio
Robert Persaud
Pilar Rivera
Serena Rivera
Sin Senh
Padmoutie Shiwsanker
Angel Soto
Leng Te
Rebecca Velasquez
Tiawanda Williams

We, the young adults of class 8L1, the Pace Academy, Junior High School 118X, the Bronx, propose that the name for Orbiter Vehicle 105 should be *Resolution.*

The name we have selected originated with the sea vessel commanded by Captain James Cook on his second and third voyages of exploration to the Pacific Ocean during the late Eighteenth Century. Captain Cook said of the *Resolution* ". . . it was the fittest for the service she was going upon of any I had ever seen."

As this sailing ship successfully explored the then almost unknown Pacific Ocean, we hope that the space shuttle *Resolution* will successfully explore the "final frontier" of space. Captain Cook's words of the Eighteenth Century, . . . "I had ambition not only to go farther than any one had been before, but as far as it was possible for man to go." . . . can easily apply to the exploration of space in the Twentieth Century.

Resolution can be defined as determination and the power of holding firmly to a purpose. By naming the new orbiter *Resolution*, we will announce to the world our determination to conquer the mysteries of the "unknown."

In addition, after the *Challenger* tragedy we believe that the selection of the name *Resolution* will show that we will never give up in our quest for furthering our knowledge of the Universe.

In conclusion, the name *Resolution* should be given to OV 105 not only to commemorate Captain Cook's voyages of exploration on a gallant ship, but because it also captures America's spirit and determination to overcome Outer Space.

Owner's Guide and Operating Manual for His Majesty's Sailing Ship Resolution

The purpose of the team's project was to show how technology has changed since the time of the sailing ship *Resolution* by writing the manual and letting the reader compare the information here with known, similar information about the Shuttle program. The students wanted to show what it would be like to be on a sailing ship and compare it to flying on a Shuttle.

The team wrote the manual as if it were the year 1772 and in a how-to style similar to a new car's operating manual. It is directly related to, calls attention to, and uses the name picked.

The P.A.C.E. Academy is a "minischool" with magnet school status within J.H.S. 118X, a public junior high school located in the Tremont section of the South Bronx. Students are selected for entrance into the academy when in grade 6 on the basis of achievement, above-average standardized test scores, interest, and performance on entrance exams, and remain in the academy for three years. The rigorous and demanding curriculum is offered for students who are academically and college oriented.

An eighth-grade literature class participated in the Orbiter-Naming Program as part of an accelerated English curriculum. In selecting an original name, students, working in committees of three to six members, not only had to do research, but had to persuade their classmates about the validity of the name and also indicate flaws in opposing viewpoints. The class, working together, wrote the persuasive statement, and committees did the research for the manual.

After the name was selected and the project decided upon, the committees determined and selected areas to be researched. In order to give them a feel for what being on a late 18th-century sailing ship was like, they viewed the film, *The Bounty.* A trip to New York City's South Street Seaport Museum, where two large sailing ships are on display, was planned for spring 1989.

Upon completing and submitting their research, the manual was typed and assembled. With an introduction from Captain James Cook addressed to his fellow countrymen, the manual includes technical information about the construction of *Resolution,* and the sails, supplies, life aboard, navigation, health care, and safety and entertainment at sea. Through their production of the booklet, the students developed a knowledge of 18th-century technology and history and were able to understand that though seemingly simple, a sailing ship was an incredibly complex piece of equipment. The contrast between a sailing ship and a Shuttle orbiter brought into sharp focus how far humanity has come in just over 200 years. At the same time, the similarities between the two helped students develop a historical perspective.

Copies of the booklets were made for each team member as well as for interested teachers to use in their classes. The team expected social studies teachers to find it particularly useful.

A Model for the Future

The booklet approach, in essence an immersion-blanket-focused approach to a topic, has potential and value for many subjects. The manual was, in fact, used by teachers in several disciplines and the team hopes their product will stimulate other teachers to emulate this method.

June, 1772

My Fellow Countrymen:

I am honored to present to you my ship, "the Resolution." At this moment she is being prepared for an important mission-to continue our exploration of the Pacific Ocean. We especially want to sail south of Australia and New Zealand; the mystery of whether land exists in the Southern Pacific Ocean must be solved.

The "Resolution" is well equiped to complete this mission, indeed, she represents the latest in 18th Century sailing technology.

It is my ambition to go further than anyone has ever been. The name of this ship captures the spirit of that ambition.

To successfully complete the expedition, we are including many important people on my staff: astronomers, naturalists, landscape painters, and scientists. We hope to gather much information.

The "Resolution" is properly equipped and supplied to overcome any obstacle that comes in the way of completing our mission. I am very confident of my ship and my crew.

This "Owner's Guide and Operating Manual" has been prepared for you-to help you under stand both the "Resolution" and our mission.

I remain, your obedient servant-

Captain James Cook

- 1 -

Introduction to Owner's Guide and Operating Manual for His Majesty's Sailing Ship *Resolution*.

Victoria

MAGELLAN PASSING HIS STRAIT (*from De Bry*).

Illustration from The Life of
Ferdinand Magellan *by Dr.
F. H. H. Guillemard.
London: George Philip &
Son, 1890. Courtesy of
Library of Congress.*

Why *Victoria*

ALLIANCE HIGH SCHOOL
400 Glamorgan Street
Alliance, Ohio 44601

David Eric Hanson
Team Coordinator
College Preparation
Biology, Chemistry,
and Genetics Teacher

TEAM MEMBERS
GRADES 9-11

Chris Blaser (10)
Jim Bussard (9)
Gregory Carter (11)
Kimberly Gibson (10)
Michael Kaminski (11)
Tod Lackey (10)
Norman Lunde (11)
Kristina Roose (11)

The spirit and soul of the American space program has been to persevere, overcome obstacles when they arise, build on adversity, and finally emerge victorious. We could find no ship that symbolizes this spirit more than *Victoria*. As far as we have determined, *Victoria* was first applied to one of the five ships in Ferdinand Magellan's historic expedition. His was a voyage of bitter hardship—and triumph. Of the five ships that began the expedition, the flagship *Trinidad, San Antonio, Concepcion, Victoria,* and *Santiago,* only *Victoria* completed the voyage around the world. . . . During the voyage Magellan discovered the strait at the tip of South America which now bears his name. It was his journey through this treacherous strait which led him to name Balboa's relatively calm "South Sea" with the more descriptive appellation "Pacific". Until *Victoria's* circumnavigation of the globe, map makers of that day believed the "South Sea" (Pacific Ocean) was rather narrow compared to the Atlantic. This mistaken belief almost cost Magellan his ships and crews—he was not prepared for the months at sea required to cross the Pacific. *Victoria's* voyage proved that the world was indeed round, that the Pacific Ocean was far more vast than anyone of the day had imagined, and that a day is lost upon sailing around the world from east to west. The voyage was an unprecedented feat of navigation.

Many parallels can be drawn between the voyage of *Victoria* and the Space Shuttle program. Some are minor and inconsequential; for example, Magellan's *Victoria,* the last of his fleet, weighed 95 tons—the shuttle *Victoria,* the last of her breed, will weigh a little over 95 tons. Other factors played a far larger role in our choice of this name. As with Magellan's voyage, our shuttle program has seen smooth sailing and success but we have also experienced setbacks and bitter hardship. But as Magellan's *Victoria* triumphed, so will we. We will continue to build on our failures as well as our victories. NASA had to convince Congress that "sailing" around the world in space was economically worthwhile, much as Magellan persuaded Spain. When NASA did obtain funding, it was insufficient to build the shuttle they had envisioned. So our space agency created what it could with the funds the government provided. The shuttle fleet is a far cry from Magellan's leaky wooden ships but a more sophisticated model would have been possible with more funding. The Shuttle program was plagued with problems, delays and other difficulties from the start. Many doubters said it would never fly, and when it did, they questioned its utility. Magellan had his detractors too. His largest ship, the *San Antonio,* turned back before entering what we now call the Strait of Magellan because its crew felt Magellan's goal was unattainable and the risk too great. Magellan contended with foul weather, which cost him *Santiago* near the tip of South America. Ironically, it was foul weather which cost the United States the shuttle *Challenger.* In the attempt to realize his dream, Magellan lost his life.

He was killed in the Philippines before he could complete the journey, but *Victoria* survived and returned to Spain. . . . We believe that just as Magellan's *Victoria* finished its difficult voyage, so will America's Shuttle *Victoria* finish her voyages and close the shuttle era successfully.

The name *Victoria* has earned a special place in history. The vessel which first bore that name achieved a victory for mankind: the first circumnavigation of the earth. It opened the doorway for many vessels and crews to follow. The shuttle *Victoria* will continue to bring scientific and economic triumphs to mankind and will also be the stepping stone to even greater use and exploration of our universe. OV-105 will be a victory for the United States space program. *Victoria* made many important discoveries as it sailed around the earth and the shuttle *Victoria* will continue to make new and important discoveries as it orbits around our planet.

Victoria, A Board Game

The team from Alliance High School developed a board game, Victoria. It is a comprehensive game about the exploration of Earth, the oceans, and the solar system.

The word "victory" implies winning a contest. The game is a race between individual players or teams to launch a Shuttle, achieve orbit, deploy the mission's six satellites, overcome unforeseen difficulties (if any arise), and land safely. It is also an educational game—a game of knowledge and recall. *Victoria* circled the globe; the players in this contest also circle the globe.

One category in the game involves Earth-exploration questions, several of which are connected to Magellan's historic expedition and man's first triumphant circumnavigation of Earth by *Victoria*. In this category are questions not only about *Victoria* but any other sea vessel that the team considered to be a possible name for the new Shuttle, as well as the vessels that already have orbiters named after them, *Discovery, Atlantis, Columbia,* and *Challenger.*

The overriding goal while developing the game was to make it both an educational and entertaining experience; the team considered it a victory for other young people and adults if they learned more about our space program and past explorations of Earth and had fun doing it. The students were well aware that some other nations are stressing science and technology more than we are in the United States. One of their challenges was to create hundreds of questions that would not overwhelm a player. They reasoned that if their project could create an interest in exploration, science, and the space program, that would be the most important victory of all.

At the beginning, most of the team felt their project would be primarily science-related, but in reality it involved as much history, English, and literature as science.

- Their first research on vessels' names involved European history, history of the New World, and history of exploration of the seas and poles.

- When they began to write questions for the different categories, they branched out in all directions. The science fiction category involved literature, movies, and television. The science category stimulated interest in the sciences and included questions from physics, astronomy, aerodynamics, chemistry, life sciences, history of science, and prominent figures in those sciences. The names and terms category included language of exploration, names, acronyms, and "space slang."

- They had input from surveys from history, math, physics, English, biology, and government classes. Some of the teachers made assignments with these surveys: For example, a math teacher had his students look up and explain equations involved in successfully orbiting a spacecraft; a biology teacher had his classes research and explain the effects of microgravity on humans or medical spinoffs from the space program.

Working on the project taught the students responsibility. They learned they had a responsibility to themselves and to the team. They learned the value of delegating responsibility and received valuable experience in committee work.

Model for the Future

The game can be adapted to any subject: an English class could study literary journeys such as the Odyssey, a government class could study the concept of a joint mission to Mars and its implications, and an economics class could determine the cost/return of various explorations. It is adaptable to any age group by altering the difficulty level of the questions, and the rules can be modified to alter length, complexity, or the goal of the game; to increase the number of players; or to balance their skill levels.

Endeavour

Pohutukawa blossom
(Metrosideros excelsa),
botanical drawing made by
Sydney Parkinson on Cook's
first voyage. Courtesy of The
Natural History Museum,
London.

Why *Endeavour*

LEXINGTON HIGH SCHOOL
2463 Augusta Highway
Lexington,
South Carolina 29072

Cathy S. Scott
Team Coordinator
Mathematics and Physics
Teacher, Grades 10-12

TEAM MEMBERS
GRADES 9-10

Janet Bainer (9)
Megan Brooks (10)
Kerry Brown (9)
Brian Derrick (9)
Sherry Hyatt (10)
Shawn Rogers (10)
Drew Varner (9)

Endeavour is a highly suitable name for OV 105. It is easy to pronounce for radio transmission, it is the namesake of a sea vessel used for research and exploration, and it captures the spirit of America's mission in space.

Endeavour means "a serious determined effort" or "to strive to achieve." This definition embodies not only the spirit of the American space program, but also the spirit of the men and women who founded and developed this country. From the early explorers, to the westward pioneer, to the scientists and explorers who traveled to the poles and to the depths of the oceans, to the astronauts in our space program, the desire to look beyond the known and to extend man's knowledge has been a driving force behind our country's growth.

Captain James Cook and his crew also demonstrated these qualities on their voyage aboard the *Endeavour.* Their two-fold mission was both exploratory and scientific. They successfully observed the transit of Venus across the face of the sun and recorded a journal about the people and customs of Tahiti. As the first great exploration of the southern Pacific Ocean, many charts and soundings were made of the Society Islands, New Zealand, and Australia.

Although Cook's quest to discover the great Southern Continent was not successful, the journey did lead to other important developments. These included the claiming of Australia and New Zealand for Britain and the study of good nutrition as a means of preventing scurvy.

Like many pioneers, Cook's journey was not always easy. A hole torn in the side of the ship by the Great Reef off Australia's coast demanded ingenuity, commitment, and dedication of the crew in order to complete the return trip to England. Unfortunately, the homecoming was saddened by the death of forty crew members from tropical diseases that were acquired in the East Indies.

The goals and accomplishments of the *Endeavour's* voyage strongly correlate with those of the American space program. Its mission, also, is two-fold: exploratory and scientific. Not only have experiments been successfully completed in space but discoveries made on earth for the space program have proven to be valuable in our everyday lives.

Just as the *Endeavour* faced problems that required innovative solutions, so has the space program. Likewise, both have known the tragedy of the loss of human life. But, as Captain Cook surmounted his obstacles and went on to further voyages, so too, has the shuttle program.

Therefore, the definition of the word, endeavour, and the spirit of the crew aboard the sea vessel *Endeavour,* make *Endeavour* an excellent choice as the name for OV 105.

A Multifaceted Project

All segments of the team's project were based upon the name *Endeavour:* A narrated slide presentation about the Space Shuttle program and the derivation of the orbiters' names, a motorized model of the Space Shuttle *Endeavour,* a model of the sea vessel *Endeavour,* a futuristic play about a flight of the orbiter *Endeavour,* and word games using space program terminology.

Slide Presentation

With permission to use pictures from NASA, the Woods Hole Oceanographic Institute, *The State* newspaper, and the University of South Carolina observatory, with photos using home and school objects, and with computer-made slides, the team developed a slide presentation about the Space Shuttle fleet. To give their script a polished touch, the students asked a retired TV anchorman to do the narration; he graciously agreed and included license-free music that was at his disposal.

Model of the orbiter *Endeavour* (6 feet long with a 6-foot wingspan)

- Built a rectangular wooden frame with scrap lumber.

- Molded a wire frame (wire gauge a little heavier than chicken wire) for the nose, wings, and tail, and a cover for the seat area for when the vehicle is not in use.

- Covered wire with layers of white garbage bags for the exterior.

- Completed black details with black garbage bags: Right wing—NASA in 3-inch capital letters, Endeavour in 2-inch letters; left wing—USA in 3-inch capital letters, an American flag.

- Attached front wheels and handle from a toy wagon (handle extends upward through a slit cut in the wooden frame to permit steering of the vehicle); attached an old caster wheel to the left rear of the vehicle and a used electrical motor wheel to the right rear.

- Inserted a molded seat from an old riding lawn mower.

- Plugged the vehicle into a long extension cord and "took off!"

A Space Shuttle glider (for younger children) was designed and built from posterboard. The team wrote instructions and drew a pattern for making it.

Model of Cook's *Endeavour*

- Made a posterboard hull and deck and spray-painted them brown.

- Used wooden dowel rods for masts.

- Rolled up paper napkins from the cafeteria for sails and used thread for rigging.

- Made cannons from strips of black construction paper, which were rolled up and pushed out to a point with a pencil tip.

- Wrote detailed instructions with drawings for reproducing this ship model.

Model for the Future

The team felt that their project showed that information about the space program can be incorporated easily into any curriculum within a school. The narrated slide video can be used in a history, geography, or science class. All the information is self-contained in the audio cassette and can be used in the listening center of a library or with people who are visually impaired. Making a slide presentation also would be a good project for a high school photography class.

Writing a narrative script or a play is a great assignment for an English or creative writing class. The drama class could present the finished product, and the art department could make scenery and props. The model ship, *Endeavour*, would be a good individual or small-group project in art or history.

The replica of the Space Shuttle could be built by a science or a vocational class. Younger students might want to build the Shuttle and use a pull rope instead of attaching a motor. Older students might want to design their own propulsion system!

They hope other teachers will enjoy the projects in their classrooms and that their ideas will inspire many more creative applications of the space program in their schools.

Godspeed

Godspeed. *Courtesy of Jamestown-Yorktown Foundation, Williamsburg, Virginia.*

Why *Godspeed*

BAYLOR SCHOOL
P.O. Box 1337
Willliams Ferry Road
Chattanooga, Tennessee
37401

Donna A. Berry
Team Coordinator
Physics Teacher
Grades 11-12

TEAM MEMBERS

Beth Hodges (12)
Jim Jackson (11)
Dexter Reid (11)
Heath Umback (11)

Four months out of England, on May 13, 1607, the *Godspeed* landed in the New World, planting the seed of the United States of America on the western shore of the Atlantic Ocean. The first successful expedition of this time, the *Godspeed* essentially began colonization in America. As Americans, we have a duty to carry on its quest for adventure by exploring another New World. Outer space holds the future; all we need to do is reach for it and it will be ours.

The *Godspeed* owned by "Merchant Adventure for the Discovery of Regions Unknown," was on a small military expedition which overcame obstacles of land, hunger, sickness, Indians, and inexperiences of governing councils to establish the most important city in Virginia, Jamestown. The love of adventure, a strong sense of patriotism, and desire for advancement compelled 52 men to face such a challenge.

Showing true patriotism for the exploration of the unknown, we believe that the name *Godspeed* should grace the next space shuttle. . . . The *Godspeed* could plant yet another seed of colonization in space, as it did in Jamestown, Virginia, in 1607.

Space Colonization

In their project the team attempted to show the importance and the inevitable colonization of space. They felt that, just as the pilgrims traveled from England to the New World, the people of the United States one day will travel and establish colonies in space.

The first step in their task of naming the new Space Shuttle began in the school library. After saying goodbye to their teammates, they individually set out to pursue the perfect name for the new OV-105. Amidst the vast array of books and periodicals, one team member found the perfect name, *Godspeed*.

They instantly knew that *Godspeed* was the name for them. *Godspeed* was one of three ships that began the colonization of the New World, and the orbiter *Godspeed* will begin colonization of space. Because they felt that both space travel and space colonization are important aspects for the future, the team used these ideas to establish five objectives:

■ To show the history of the ship's name in relation to the history of colonization;

■ To familiarize students with the physical appearance of their proposed spacecraft;

■ To learn about the Shuttle's liftoff procedure;

- To teach students about future space colonies—how they will look and the uses they will serve—and what will be involved in building and stocking a space colony;

- To learn about organization and team effort.

Their research included interviews with teachers, parents, fellow students, and librarians for both ideas and information. Preparation included discussions about different ways to link their wide variety of topics and gathering various tools and supplies. Class discussions involved the history of the first *Godspeed* and the current Space Shuttle, the advantages and disadvantages of space colonization, and how living would be effected in space.

The project became a handsome series of pictures, posters, drawings, and models organized into three sections:

1 Space Colony

The first section is an array of mounted photographs illustrating how space can be colonized and the team's ideas about future space settlements. They organized the pictures to show the basic needs of colonists in space: food, clothing, and sleeping arrangements. Pictures of food show the present technology used in preparing meals for Shuttle flights; clothing for inside and outside the orbiter; and sleeping arrangements to accommodate "weightlessness."

2 Colonization

In order to express their idea of building a space colony, the students wanted to depict *Godspeed's* voyage from England to America and the orbiter's voyage from America to space. With Legos, "the universal building blocks," they built a model of their spaceship and bought a model kit for a Space Shuttle. To show the complexities of building a space colony, they used Legos again to create two possible colonies. Building with the Legos was the most challenging part of the project. Lacking the "right parts," they improvised their spacecraft using parts of different colors and mismatched shapes. In addition to the two models, they made a poster to show the inside of the Space Shuttle and the space colonies.

3 Liftoff

Again using a poster, they compiled pictures to demonstrate the Space Shuttle's launch sequence. It includes a crew patch the team designed showing the early exploration of Jamestown with the original *Godspeed* and the exploration of tomorrow with the new orbiter.

Although their project grew from a requirement in their physics class—to take some aspect of physics in space and relate it to everday life—the students recognized how many other fields of study were involved as they used history in researching their ship, math in studying the Space Shuttle, and art in creating their project.

The team felt their project also taught them many valuable lessons useful for their future lives: teamwork, organization, and how to use their time in the most efficient way.

Model for the Future

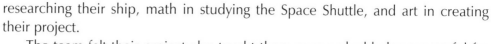

The *Godspeed* team wanted their project to be not only an enjoyable experience for themselves, but a learning tool for future students. Because everyone has Legos or household products with which to build models, the team felt that by using such items for a similar project, students would understand the complexities and tedious efforts involved in designing and building a space colony. It also would be an opportunity to integrate several disciplines into a large composite project.

Chatham

Model of HMS Chatham.
*Courtesy of Oregon
Historical Society, #OrHi
37302, Portland.*

Why *Chatham*

STEVENSON HIGH SCHOOL

P.O. Box 430

Stevenson,
Washington 98648

*Leslie R. Hastings
Team Coordinator
Mathematics and Science
Teacher, Grades 9-12*

TEAM MEMBERS

*Arnold Alcantar (12)
Christopher Allinger (11)
Karl Bach (12)
Shyler Brannan (11)
Christofer Clemens (11)
Andrew Gardner (11)
Heather Hafford (12)
Eric Hansen (12)
Scott Harrison (12)
Chris Holmes (11)
Mike Irwin (12)
Rhonda Jewell (11)
Melissa McDonnell (11)
Thad McGlinn (11)
Carrie Schenk (12)
Grant Warrick (12)*

The H.M.S. *Chatham* played an important part in the early exploration of the new world, and it also has a significant connection with two other space shuttles already commissioned and in the service of our country.

In the year of 1792, a major discovery was made by the Yankee trader, Robert Gray. That discovery was the Columbia River. This river was at first believed to be the long sought after Northwest Passage. In time it was realized that the river was not the mythical Northwest Passage; but in actuality it still played a major role in the early settlement of the Northwest. Robert Gray, in his ship *Columbia,* crossed the Columbia River bar and gave the newly formed nation, the United States, the discovery rights to this massive river. He bestowed the name of his ship, the *Columbia,* onto this new body of water.

After a short exploratory visit he recrossed the bar and sailed north. On this voyage north the namesake of a future orbiter (the *Columbia*) encountered yet another namesake of a future orbiter (the *Discovery*). This second vessel (the *Discovery*) was under the command of Admiral George Vancouver. Unlike the Yankee merchant, Robert Gray, Vancouver's main mission was that of exploration and obtaining exploratory rights for Great Britain.

When hearing of the discovery of Robert Gray, Vancouver quickly headed south with his small fleet hoping to gain some exploratory rights to this part of the new world for Great Britain. Upon arriving at the Columbia River bar, Vancouver sent the smaller ship, the H.M.S. *Chatham*, across the treacherous entrance to the new river. Lt. William R. Broughton sailed some one hundred plus miles up the Columbia River to the beginning of the scenic Columbia River Gorge. During this journey, Lt. Broughton named Mt. Hood and Mt. St. Helens (which gained much notoriety in 1980 with its eruption) after prominent British statesmen. He also named a point of land jutting out into the Columbia River, Point Vancouver, after his Admiral. This area became the present day town of Vancouver, U.S.A.

The Columbia River became a major artery for the development of our country. In 1804, President Jefferson sent his "Discovery Corp", led by Captains Lewis and Clark to explore the newly purchased Louisiana Territory and to also explore that new river of the northwest, the Columbia. A few years later the Hudson Bay Company set up headquarters at Point Vancouver and the Columbia River was then used as an inland route into Canada. After the Oregon country became a territory of the U.S., it was the Columbia River that served as one of the final pathways of the Oregon Trail, which brought settlers into the Northwest. Settlers would put into the river (on hand built rafts) at The Dalles area and continue down through dangerous rapids to their final destination, the Willamette Valley. Early explorers, such as Captain John C. Fremont, also used the Columbia River as a passageway through the high Cascades.

Because of the importance of the discovery of the Columbia River and its subsequent development into one of the sea level passages through our Northwest, we of the third period astronomy class of Stevenson feel that the name of the H.M.S. *Chatham* should be seriously considered as the name of the new orbiter, OV-105. After all it was the *Chatham* that accompanied Vancouver's *Discovery* in its epic exploration of the Northwest. It was also the *Chatham* that continued on into the Columbia, where the *Discovery* was felt not capable of going. Finally, it was the *Chatham* that did the follow up on the exploration of the Columbia River, that was left by the original *Columbia*. We would like to see these three ships united again in exploratory and scientific expeditions that would perpetuate their names in the history of mankind's next step forward.

HMS *Chatham* and the Columbia Gorge Study

The Stevenson High School team developed an interdisciplinary project related to the Columbia Gorge Study, a class that has been taught for several years. The project included geology, history, zoology, botany, trails, and management of the scenic Columbia Gorge.

The team was divided into subgroups, and each was given a task to develop objectives and activities for each portion of the curriculum. They also were given instructions to involve the community in their project, and with this in mind off they went.

Through the years, it has been the goal of the Columbia Gorge Study class to present to the students of the area information that will make them more aware and appreciative of the unique habitat in which they are living. The Columbia Gorge has been declared a national scenic area by Congress, so it is even more important now that the students have an understanding of the checks and balances that exist in the Gorge. This, in turn, will help give them a better understanding about why certain policies have to be implemented. The introduction of any additions to the curriculum that would help achieve the primary goal of the Columbia Gorge Study class would be beneficial and appreciated, especially since it would be coming from the students themselves.

■ One subgroup set off with the idea of reenacting the trip of Lt. Broughton as he traveled up the Columbia River. The logical step would be to tie in a vehicle that periodically makes the trip, such as the sternwheeler that operates during the summer months in the Columbia Gorge. The historical replica annually comes up the Columbia River in late spring. The Port of Cascade Locks (owners of the ship) were contacted; it was found that 10 passages were not booked, so the group reserved them.

- Because a sternwheeler trip was to be made, another subgroup decided that during the trip they would compare the river of today with the way it was during the time of HMS *Chatham*. Research failed to find any maps produced by Lt. Broughton; however, research did locate a map of this section of river that had been produced by the Lewis and Clark expedition. The expedition came through the area only a few years after Lt. Broughton, so most of the river area was probably the same. Coincidentally, both exploratory groups were in the same area at the same time of the year (around October 31).

- During the sternwheeler trip, another group would take responsbility for including in the curriculum a list of flora and fauna that were described by the Lewis and Clark expedition and compare it to what is found on the river today.

- A different subgroup jumped on the idea of Lt. Broughton naming natural objects such as Mount Hood, Mount St. Helens, Point Vancouver, and the Barings River (now the Sandy River). Research done by this group provided a list of the names to introduce into the curriculum.

- Another subgroup followed up on the geological aspect of the expedition. Because Lt. Broughton named Mount St. Helens and because lava activity played such a big part in the formation of the Columbia Gorge, the group felt it would be appropriate to include in the curriculum a field trip to the Mount St. Helens area. The students contacted the Mount St. Helens National Volcanic Monument headquarters and a field trip was organized as an activity for the curriculum. The field trip will be taken in the spring by all Columbia Gorge classes. It will include exploration of lava tubes and visits to interpretive sites, and will cover both the geological significance and the ecological viewpoint. The staff said they also had developed curricula for teaching about Mount St. Helens, and the team could share ideas.

Model for the Future

The curriculum developed by this program was to be introduced into the current curriculum of the Columbia Gorge Study class and evaluated by the team coordinator and the principal of Stevenson High School. The Washington State Centennial Committee of the Columbia Gorge area also was to evaluate the project because it was sponsoring two class members on the sternwheeler trip. In addition, the Columbia Gorge Scenic Area Commission expressed an interest in incorporating the team's project into the curriculum that the commission was developing for teaching a Columbia Gorge class in schools inside and outside of the Columbia Gorge area.

Deepstar

**Deepstar *4000* undergoing
shallow-water tests of
propulsion and photography
systems. Courtesy of
Oceanic Division, Westinghouse Electric Corporation,
Annapolis, Maryland.**

Why *Deepstar*

PADEN CITY
MIDDLE SCHOOL
425 South Fourth Avenue
Paden City, West Virginia
26159

Diane M. Berdar
Team Coordinator
Teacher of the Gifted
Grades 6-8

TEAM MEMBERS

Andy Chambers (7)
Jeff Mishtawy (8)
Amy Smith (8)
Melanie Stender (8)

Deepstar, a family of undersea vehicles manufactured by Westinghouse Electric Corporation, is one of the most adaptable underwater exploration vessels in the world today. *Deepstar* 2000 and *Deepstar* 4000, commonly referred to as DS-2000 and DS-4000, have features that are unique to each system.

Deepstar 2000, a 19 foot craft powered by lead-acid batteries, was the first in the *Deepstar* family. Built of steel and glass reinforced plastic, three people can travel 45 hours within its walls, conducting geographical, biological, physical, and chemical experiments. The highly sophisticated system is equipped with two remote manipulators that perform tasks similar to that of the Remote Manipulator System in a space shuttle's cargo bay. The mechanical arms of DS-2000 collect samples from ocean beds and are capable of setting up instruments for the crew.

Inside is a vast wealth of advanced technology. Some of the instruments included are: an acoustic sub-bottom profiler, side-looking sonar, a sediment sampling system, sediment and hard-rock corers, and several types of photographic equipment.

The maneuvering/propulsion system is made up of two main thrusters which perform tasks similar to the Solid Rocket Boosters on the shuttle. The two vertical thrusters are comparable to the three main engines on the rear of the shuttle; the two horizontal thrusters do virtually the same job as the Orbital-Maneuvering System. The *Deepstar* 2000 is truly a multi-faceted submersible vessel.

The *Deepstar* 4000, the sister of the DS-2000, also has wondrous exploring capabilities. Modern technology has helped to up-date its overall performance.

The DS-4000 is capable of operating at depths of 4000 feet by changing the design of the model, and by basing the change on the "Diving Saucer" concept. The hull shape was converted from ellipsoidal to spherical and by using the latest technology in high strength steel.

The tasks conducted by *Deepstar* 4000 include performing underwater observation of ocean environment and conducting underwater photography missions. In addition, the DS-4000 advances the mapping techniques of the ocean floor. Furthermore, it assists the U.S. military and commercial operations. The life-support system will provide for a pilot and two observers for up to 48 hours.

The *Deepstar* family is a true asset to underwater research and discovery.

Deepstar is an appropriate name for a spacecraft because, in exploring the heavens, we are reaching for the stars deep in space. *Deepstar* explores a sea of water, as OV-105 will soon explore a sea of stars. As *Deepstar* 2000 and 4000 continue to explore the frontier of the undersea world, the shuttle *Deepstar* will carry us into the next century of discovery in the frontier of space.

Our mission in space is to lead the world in the exploration of space; it is also to further our technology not only in space but on earth as well. It broadens our knowledge of space by making the unknown known. Indeed, by sending high-tech vehicles into space, we are proving the advanced technology of the United States of America.

The sea vessel *Deepstar* conducts numerous experiments to help mankind. This is how it captures America's mission in space.

Deepstar Competes for OV-105

For the Paden City Middle School team, *Deepstar* created an image of a cluster of stars deep in the farthest reaches of the universe. Their project centered on this theme with the creation of a multisensory experience for the audience. Using a three-sided display board, they set the stage for simulating the feeling of exploration in outer space.

The team's first objective was to locate resource books on sea vessels for screening possible names. Because theirs is a small town, the school library is somewhat limited. So they visited public libraries in nearby towns, checked their personal book collections, and then established a resource center in their classroom.

After choosing possible selections, they critiqued, as a group, each name on the basis of its background, contribution to mankind, pronunciation, and if it was appropriate for a Space Shuttle. To their dismay, they found this to be a most challenging task! They debated on several occasions and then, after searching through the *National Geographic Index*, sighted the name *Deepstar*. Within two days, they discovered more information on the name and decided to pursue it. Their nearby Westinghouse branch office located in Pittsburgh, Pennsylvania, referred them to the Oceanic Division of Westinghouse in Maryland. Supplied with updated literature on *Deepstar* and photographs of the sea vessel in action, they carefully scrutinized the information and decided *Deepstar* was their winning choice.

Next, they wrote to the NASA Langley Research Center for information on the U.S. space program. Using information from Langley, they were able to make analogies between the capabilities and instruments of *Deepstar* and the Shuttle systems.

When they learned that astronaut Jon McBride would be speaking at a nearby college, they wrote objectives for a field trip to attend the program. It was approved by the Board of Education. Exhilarated by his presentation, they decided to attempt to tie a sensory feeling into their project.

The team prepared two models of OV-105, one a model kit of *Discovery* and the other a clay model to scale. A galaxy diorama was created to give the illusion of the Shuttle exploring in the depths of space. A collage of space science pictures captured the spirit of America's mission in space by showing the

accomplishments of U.S. technology in the areas of photography, discovery, and experimentation. A diagram on poster board showed OV-105 in launching position. The magic stardust for the project was the music from the movie *Space Camp* playing in the background.

Parents acted as "cheerleaders," helped the team brainstorm ideas for the development of the project, and provided transportation to meetings held after school and to public libraries. In addition, they were "sounding boards" throughout the course of planning and making necessary adjustments and improvements. The parents also helped by providing materials for and assistance with the construction of the display.

The team invited community leaders, their Partners-in-Education (two local businesses), Board of Education members, parents, Paden City Middle School Faculty, and professionals in space science from nearby colleges to critique their project, which provided good feedback on their work. Their project was scheduled for display in January and February 1989 at the local post office, public library, their Partners-in-Education, and the Board of Education.

The students experienced a wide variety of emotions throughout the course of the project: frustration over a complicated project that, at times, seemed too large to handle; hope as they began to see their efforts materialize; then joy when a completed project stood before them. As one team member expressed it, "I learned an important lesson of confidence. When things seem hopeless, often they aren't. Reach for the stars - and sooner or later you'll touch one."

Model for the Future

The team felt that several factors give their project potential as a model for future classroom and school activities. First, it can be used to highlight other problems such as pollution, deterioration of the ozone layer, population explosion, disease, crime prevention, and substance abuse. Second, it is an ideal project for cooperative learning groups. Skills developed in this environment—positive interdependence, individual accountability, shared leadership, and shared responsibility for each other—are cooperative learning experiences that foster positive relationships and the process of peer acceptance; this makes a major contribution to the socialization of middle school students.

Nautilus

*The nuclear-powered
submarine USS Nautilus
(SSN 571) during sea trials.
U.S. NAVY PHOTOGRAPH by
ELECTRIC BOAT DIVISION.*

Why *Nautilus*

*CHEYENNE EAST
HIGH SCHOOL
2800 East Pershing Boulevard
Cheyenne, Wyoming 82001*

*Larry Dwayne Adams
Team Coordinator
Science Teacher
Grades 10-12*

TEAM MEMBERS

*Katherine Davis (11)
Jason Foist (10)
Shane Kennedy (12)
Eric Payne (10)
Nicole Pomerinke (12)
Shannelle Porter (11)
Lars Christian Story II (11)
Frank Taplin (11)*

It seems that man will never stop exploring the extremes that confront him, such as the core of the earth, the greatest depths of the oceans, the north pole and deep space. Man spends much of his time designing machines that enable him to investigate these hostile environments. Scientists and engineers, in their hopes to make dreams become reality are often inspired by great fiction writers such as Jules Verne in order to stimulate their creativity and curiosity. An example of this process is the development of the submarine. Simon Lake, a naval architect, who authored the book, *The Submarine in War and Peace*, 1918, once said, "Ever since I designed my first submarine as a boy in 1883, shortly after reading Jules Verne's *Twenty Thousand Leagues Under the Sea,* I have been impressed with the submarine's possibilities in the scientific investigation of under-sea conditions." (Lake, 1918)

One of the first purely scientific adventures undertaken by submarines, one that helped show the way to the research submersible, was the Wilkins-Ellsworth *Nautilus* Expedition of 1931. Sir Hubert Wilkins, an Australian explorer of the polar regions, had decided it was possible to reach the North Pole under the ice by submarine as suggested by his friend and co-explorer, Vilhjalmur Stefansson (Stefansson, 1932). . . . Wilkins was convinced that significant scientific contribution could be made by this dangerous voyage. Such measurements as the bathymetry of the Arctic Ocean (the measurement in ocean depth), magnetic and gravity observations, and the collection of water samples from various depths were among the goals of the expedition. Wilkins believed it might be possible to set up weather observation stations near the pole (Wilkins, 1931).

The *Nautilus* submarine was taken out of moth balls and converted for Arctic service. She was 175 feet long (approximately 53 feet longer than the Space Shuttle) with an 18 foot beam . . . . On March 24, 1931 the *Nautilus,* christened in honor of Jules Verne by Jules Verne's grandson, set sail for the North Pole. . . . The ship came within 500 miles . . . .

The U.S.S. *Nautilus* was the first nuclear powered submarine thanks to the inspiration of Admiral Hyman George Rickover who wanted it to advance the technology for the new generation. On June 8, 1958, Commander William Anderson was informed that the U.S.S. *Nautilus* would go to England by way of the North Pole. Project Sunshine (code name) was put into effect the next day as they headed for the polar cap. . . . On June 17, 1958 the U.S.S. *Nautilus* had to turn around and go back to Hawaii due to the discovery of several icebergs and damage to the main periscope.

The crew had few problems on the way to the pole the second time. . . . On August 3, 1958 the first underwater sea vessel reached the North Pole, 90 degrees north. (Anderson, 1959)

The name *Nautilus* will always live on, thanks to Jules Verne, Sir Hubert Wilkins, Lincoln Ellsworth, Harald Sverdrup, Captain Anderson, Admiral

Hyman George Rickover and many others. For these men were true heroes, courageous examples that inspire dreams of new adventures.

The space shuttle OV-105 should be named the *Nautilus* for many reasons. The *Nautilus* has a very interesting past, from the fictional submarine in Jules Verne's *20,000 Leagues Under the Sea,* to the first expedition to reach under the North Pole by a submersible. These relatively new sea-going vessels have carried man to new frontiers of scientific research and exploration. Like the space shuttle, these machines were designed to transport man through environments not well suited for him. But as man continues to dream and explore, he will leave his home to find new frontiers and adventures. The *Nautilus* is an appropriate name reflecting this spirit.

Project Sunshine, An Adventure in Philately

The name *Nautilus* was chosen by the members of the Cheyenne East High School Science Club. Wanting to express the vessel's rich history in a creative way, the team decided on the creation of U. S. commemorative postage stamps that would be submitted to the Postmaster General and the National Stamp Committee if the new Shuttle were named the *Nautilus.*

The theme of their project, The Significance of Exploration, was inspired by Wilkins' book, *Under the North Pole.* Their series of commemorative stamps would show the significance of *Nautilus* as a sea vessel used in research and exploration, from literary fiction to scientific fact. The display of *Nautilus* vessels would be designed to illustrate the historical chronology. The art work in each stamp would show *Nautilus* in the northern part of the hemisphere among the waters where the vessels were submerged in the depths of different oceans and the orbiter *Nautilus* shown monitoring the Northern Hemisphere in the ocean of space.

Through research and study, the team realized that fiction played an important role in shaping the thoughts of future scientists and explorers. This process was illustrated in Anderson's book, *Nautilus-90-North,* that vividly recreated life aboard the world's first nuclear submarine. The suspense of Top Secret orders, the human and humorous incidents that helped the crew pass time, and the unparalleled adventure and exploration of the first probe of the Wilkins-Ellsworth submarine expedition that came within 500 miles of the North Pole and fulfilled the Jules Verne dream in steaming *20,000 Leagues Under the Sea* are contained in Anderson's book.

The proposal to develop commemorative stamps integrated various disciplines into a single focus. This not only included the traditional disciplines, but led the team to more specific areas such as philately, drafting, and cartography.

When the team wanted public reaction to their name, community support came in the form of a billboard that announced the Orbiter-Naming Program and

the team's proposal. Positive input came from throughout the Cheyenne area. Next, five members of the team visited The Unicover Corporation for information about the creation of postage stamps and recommendations that would enhance their project. They also visited the First Day Cover Museum in Cheyenne. Many libraries and archives in the region supported their study, and parents, relatives, and student alumni contributed crucial advice, materials, and financial aid.

A Model for the Future

Educators are always looking for new methods for encouraging interdisciplinary learning. In this particular model, a number of disciplines were focused into a single goal with the creation of commemorative stamps. It is a type of focused activity that can be applied in almost any classroom at any level. Stamps are used to commemorate major achievements in history. While the study of stamps is not exactly a typical academic subject, in this project, which enabled students to design their own stamps, the study generated a real excitement for the Orbiter-Naming Program.

The National Stamp Committee approves between 60 and 120 commemorative stamps a year. The ability to get students involved in designing a stamp that will be used by all people in the United States offers the kind of challenge and excitement that provides the additional motivation to make this educational model an ongoing annual national program.

Bibliography

In addition to the *Readers' Guide to Periodical Literature*, standard encyclopedias and dictionaries, biographies, and general histories, several teams listed the following books as helpful in researching their names and formulating their projects.

Alexander, Tom, *Project Apollo, Man to the Moon.* New York: Harper & Row, 1964.

Allen, Joseph P., *Entering Space: An Astronaut's Odyssey.* New York: Stewart, Tabori & Chang, 1984.

Allen, Oliver E., *The Pacific Navigators.* Alexandria, VA: Time-Life Books, Inc., 1980.

Allen, Oliver E., *The Windjammers.* Alexandria, VA: Time-Life Books, 1978.

Anderson, W. R., Commander, U.S.N., *Nautilus-90-North.* Cleveland: World Publishing Company, 1959.

Angelucci, Enzo and Attilio Cucari, *Ships.* New York: Greenwich House, 1983.

Armstrong, Richard, *A History of Seafaring, Volume II: The Discoverers.* New York: Praeger Publishers, 1969.

Bendick, Jeanne, *Space Travel.* New York: F. Watts, 1982.

Bergaust, Erik and William Foss, *Oceanographers In Action.* Toronto: Longmans Canada Ltd., 1968.

Briggs, Peter, *Laboratory at the Bottom of the World.* New York: David McKay Company, Inc., 1970.

Brosse, Jacques, *Great Voyages of Discovery: Circumnavigators and Scientists, 1764-1843.* Paris: Bordas, 1983.

Brower, Norman J., *International Register of Historic Ships.* Annapolis: Naval Institute Press, 1985.

Burgess, Robert F., *Ships Beneath the Sea: A history of subs and submersibles.* New York: McGraw-Hill, 1975.

Cave, Ronald, *Space Shuttle.* New York: The Gloucester Press, 1982.

Chant, Christopher, *Space Shuttle.* Hong Kong: McLaren Publishing, 1984.

Clarke, Arthur C., *Life Science Library: Man and Space.* New York: Time-Life Books, 1968.

Collins, Michael, *Liftoff: The Story of America's Adventure in Space.* New York: Grove Press, 1988.

Cooper, Henry S., *Before Liftoff.* Baltimore: Johns Hopkins, 1987.

Cosgrave, J. II, *America Sails the Seas.* Boston: Houghton Mifflin, 1962.

Cousteau, Jacques-Yves, *Calypso.* New York: Harry N. Abrams, 1983.

Cousteau, Jacques-Yves, *The Ocean World of Jacques Cousteau, The Series.* London: Angus and Robertson, 1973.

David, Heather M., *Admiral Rickover and the Nuclear Navy.* New York: Putnam, 1970.

Deepstar 4000. Annapolis: Westinghouse Electric Corporation, Underseas Division, Ocean Research and Engineering Laboratory.

Deepstar/Searchstar: Research Submersible System. Annapolis: Westinghouse Electric Corporation, Underseas Division, Ocean Research Laboratory, June 1971.

DeLong, G. W. and E. DeLong, *The Voyage of the* Jeannette, *The Ship and Ice Journals of George W. DeLong, Lieutenant-Commander U.S.N., and Commander of the Polar Expedition of 1879-1881,* Vols. I and II. New York: Houghton Mifflin, 1983.

Dicerto, Joseph J., *Star Voyage.* New York: Julian Messner, 1981.

Dugan, James, *Undersea Explorer.* New York: The Gloucester Press, 1983.

Fichter, George S., *The Space Shuttle.* New York: The Gloucester Press, 1983.

Finney, Ben R., *Hōkuleʻa: The Way to Tahiti.* New York: Dodd, Mead and Company, 1979.

Genett, Ann, *Aviation.* Minneapolis: Dillon Press, Inc., 1977.

Hawkes, Nigel, *Space Shuttle.* New York: The Gloucester Press, 1983.

Haws, Duncan, *Ships and the Sea: A Chronological Review.* New York: Crescent Books, 1976.

Joels, Kerry Mark and Gregory P. Kennedy, *The Space Shuttle Operator's Manual.* New York: Ballantine Books, 1982.

Kelley, Kevin W., ed., *The Home Planet.* Reading, MA: Addison-Wesley, 1988.

Kerrod, Robin, *The Illustrated History of NASA: Anniversary Edition.* New York: Gallery Books, 1986.

Kummer, Frederic A., *Erikson the Lucky.* Chicago: John C. Winston Company, 1936.

Laing, Alexander, *American Ships.* New York: American Heritage Press, 1971.

Maddocks, Melvin, *The Great Liners.* Alexandria, VA: Time-Life Books, 1978.

Mason, Robert Grant, ed., *Life in Space.* Alexandria, VA.: Time-Life Books, 1983.

McGrath, Patrick, *The Lewis and Clark Expedition.* Morristown, NJ: Silver Burdett Company, 1985.

Mendell, W. W., ed., *Lunar Bases and Space Activities of the 21st Century.* Houston: Lunar and Planetary Institute, 1985.

Moore, Patrick, *Guide to Mars.* New York: Norton and Co., 1977.

National Aeronautics and Space Administration, *NASA Highlights: 1986-1988.* Washington, DC: Government Printing Office, 1988.

National Aeronautics and Space Administration, *NASA, The First 25 Years, 1958-1983: A Resource for Teachers.* Washington, DC: Government Printing Office, 1983.

Preiss, Byron, ed., *The Universe.* New York: Bantam Books, 1987.

Rey, H. A., *The Stars: A New Way to See Them.* Boston, Houghton Mifflin, 1980.

Ride, Sally K., *Leadership and America's Future in Space: A Report to the Administrator.* Washington, DC: National Aeronautics and Space Administration, 1987.

Ride, Sally and Susan Okie, *To Space And Back.* New York: Lothrop, Lee & Shepard Books, 1986.

Ross, Frank, Jr., *Model Satellites and Spacecraft.* New York: Lothrop, Lee & Shepard Company, 1969.

Rugoff, Milton, *Marco Polo's Adventures in China.* New York: American Heritage Publishing Company, 1964.

Schulke, Flip, Debra, and Penelope, and Raymond McPhee, *Your Future in Space.* New York: Crown Publishers, Inc., 1986.

Short, Nicholas, M., et al., *Mission to Earth: Landsat Views the World.* Washington, DC: Government Printing Office, 1979.

Stambler, Irwin, *Space Ship: The Story of the X-15.* New York: Putnam, 1970.

The Report by the National Commission on Space, *Pioneering the Space Frontier.* New York: Bantam Books, 1986.

Truly, Richard H., *Space Shuttle: The Journey Continues.* Washington, DC: National Aeronautics and Space Administration.

Vogt, Gregory, *Space Vehicles.* New York: F. Watts, 1987.

Von Braun, Wernher, *History of Rocketry and Space Travel.* Chicago: J.G. Ferguson Publishing Company, 1986.

Von Braun, Wernher and Frederick I. Ordway, *Space Travel: A History.* New York: Harper & Row, 1975.

Ward, Ralph T., *Steamboats: A history of early adventure.* Indianapolis: The Bobbs-Merrill Company, Inc., 1973.

Warner, Oliver, *Captain Cook and the South Pacific.* New York: American Heritage Publishing Company, Inc., 1963.

Whipple, A. B. C., *The Clipper Ships.* Alexandria, VA: Time-Life Books, 1980.

Wilcox, Desmond, *Ten Who Dared.* Boston: Little, Brown, and Company, 1975.

Appendices

Appendix A

1988 Council of Chief State School Officers

GORDON M. AMBACH, EXECUTIVE DIRECTOR

Wayne Teague
Superintendent of Education
State Department of Education
Alabama

William G. Demmert
Commissioner of Education
State Department of Education
Alaska

Fuaileleo Pita Sunia
Director of Education
Department of Education
American Samoa

C. Diane Bishop
Superintendent of Public Instruction
State Department of Education
Arizona

Ruth Steele
Director, General Education Division
State Department of Education
Arkansas

Bill Honig
Superintendent of Public Instruction
State Department of Education
California

William T. Randall
Commissioner of Education
State Department of Education
Colorado

Gerald N. Tirozzi
Commissioner of Education
State Department of Education
Connecticut

William B. Keene
Superintendent of Public Instruction
State Department of Public
    Instruction
Delaware

John Stremple
Director
Office of Dependents Schools
Department of Defense

Floretta Dukes McKenzie
Superintendent of Public Schools
District of Columbia

Betty Castor
Commissioner of Education
State Department of Education
Florida

Werner Rogers
Superintendent of Schools
State Department of Education
Georgia

Gloria Nelson
Director of Education
Department of Education
Guam

Charles T. Toguchi
Superintendent of Education
Department of Education
Hawaii

Jerry L. Evans
Superintendent of Public Instruction
State Department of Education
Idaho

Ted Sanders
Superintendent of Education
State Board of Education
Illinois

H. Dean Evans
Superintendent of Public Instruction
State Department of Education
Indiana

William L. Lepley
Director of Education
State Department of Education
Iowa

Lee Droegemueller
Commissioner of Education
State Department of Education
Kansas

John H. Brock
Superintendent of Public Instruction
State Department of Education
Kentucky

Thomas G. Clausen
Superintendent of Education
State Department of Education
Louisiana

Eve M. Bither
Commissioner of Education
Department of Educational and
    Cultural Services
Maine

David W. Hornbeck
State Superintendent of Schools
State Department of Education
Maryland

Harold Raynolds, Jr.
Commissioner of Education
State Department of Education
Massachusetts

Gary D. Hawks
Acting Superintendent of Public
    Instruction
State Department of Education
Michigan

Ruth E. Randall
Commissioner of Education
State Department of Education
Minnesota

Richard A. Boyd
Superintendent of Education
State Department of Education
Mississippi

Robert E. Bartman
Commissioner of Education
Department of Elementary
    and Secondary Education
Missouri

Ed Argenbright
Superintendent of Public Instruction
State Office of Public Instruction
Montana

Joseph E. Lutjeharms
Commissioner of Education
State Department of Education
Nebraska

Eugene T. Paslov
Superintendent of Public Instruction
State Department of Education
Nevada

John T. MacDonald
Commissioner of Education
State Department of Education
New Hampshire

Saul Cooperman
Commissioner of Education
State Department of Education
New Jersey

Alan Morgan
Superintendent of Public Instruction
State Department of Education
New Mexico

Thomas Sobol
Commissioner of Education
State Education Department
New York

A. Craig Phillips
Superintendent of Public Instruction
State Department of Public Instruction
North Carolina

Wayne G. Sanstead
Superintendent of Public Instruction
State Department of Public Instruction
North Dakota

Henry I. Sablan
Commissioner of Education
Department of Education
Commonwealth of the Northern
    Mariana Islands

Franklin B. Walter
Superintendent of Public Instruction
State Department of Education
Ohio

John M. Folks
Superintendent of Public Instruction
State Department of Education
Oklahoma

Verne A. Duncan
Superintendent of Public Instruction
State Department of Education
Oregon

Thomas K. Gilhool
Secretary of Education
State Department of Education
Pennsylvania

Awilda Aponte Roque
Secretary of Education
Department of Education
Puerto Rico

Troy Earhart
Commissioner of Education
State Department of Education
Rhode Island

Charlie G. Williams
State Superintendent of Education
State Department of Education
South Carolina

Henry Kosters
Secretary of Education
Department of Education and
    Cultural Affairs
South Dakota

Charles E. Smith
Commissioner of Education
State Department of Education
Tennessee

William N. Kirby
Commissioner of Education
Texas Education Agency
Texas

James R. Moss
Superintendent of Public Instruction
State Office of Education
Utah

Richard P. Mills
Commissioner of Education
State Department of Education
Vermont

S. John Davis
Superintendent of Public Instruction
State Department of Education
Virginia

Linda Creque
Commissioner of Education
Department of Education
Virgin Islands

Frank B. Brouillet
Superintendent of Public Instruction
State Department of Public
Instruction
Washington

Thomas McNeel
State Superintendent of Schools
State Department of Education
West Virginia

Herbert J. Grover
Superintendent of Public Instruction
State Department of Public
    Instruction
Wisconsin

Lynn O. Simons
State Superintendent of Public
    Instruction
State Department of Education
Wyoming

**Non-Council members who
participated in the Orbiter-Naming
Program**

Ed Brown
Assistant Secretary
Bureau of Indian Affairs
Department of Interior

Ernest Mannino
Director of Overseas Schools
Department of State

Appendix B

State-Level Coordinators

The following state education agency personnel adminstered their respective Orbiter-Naming Program competitions.

ALABAMA
William C. Ward
Coordinator, Elementary Services
State Department of Education

ALASKA
Sandra Barry
Recognition Programs Coordinator
State Department of Education

AMERICAN SAMOA
Rick Davis
Science Coordinator
Department of Education

ARIZONA
Carl E. Beisecker
Program Specialist
State Department of Education

ARKANSAS
Bill Fulton
State Science Supervisor
State Department of Education

BUREAU OF INDIAN AFFAIRS
Bill Mehojah
Chief, Branch of Elementary and
    Secondary Education

CALIFORNIA
Gayland Jordan
Consultant, Math Science Unit
State Department of Education

COLORADO
Robert Stack
Science Consultant
State Department of Education

CONNECTICUT
Sigmund Abeles, Ph.D.
Science Consultant
State Department of Education

DELAWARE
Bud Hagarty, Ph.D.
Public Information Officer
State Department of Public
    Instruction

DEPARTMENT OF DEFENSE
Marvin Kurtz
Social Studies Coordinator
Office of Dependents Schools

DEPARTMENT OF STATE
Bob Ferguson
Educational Officer of Near East
    and South Asia

DISTRICT OF COLUMBIA
Michon Peck
Assistant Director, Student Affairs
District of Columbia Public Schools

FLORIDA
Cynthia Perkins
Program Specialist IV
State Department of Education

GEORGIA
Eleanor Gilmer
State Department of Education

GUAM
John A. Simpson
School Program Consultant
Department of Education

HAWAII
John Hawkins
Science Education, OIS
Department of Education

IDAHO
Lindy High
Public Information Officer
State Department of Education

ILLINOIS
Lee Milner
Special Assistant for Public Affairs
State Board of Education

INDIANA
Joe Wright
Aerospace Education, Office of
    School Assistance
State Department of Education

IOWA
Joseph Wolvek, Ph.D.
Consultant
State Department of Education

KANSAS
Warren Bell
Director of State and Federal
    Administration
State Department of Education

KENTUCKY
Paul Mauer
Consultant
State Department of Education

LOUISIANA
Shelby Boudreaux
Education Specialist
State Department of Education

MAINE
Thomas Keller
Science Consultant
Department of Educational and
    Cultural Services

MARYLAND
Louise Tanney
Specialist
State Department of Education

MASSACHUSETTS
George Perry and Marylou Anderson
State Department of Education

MICHIGAN
Ellen C. Cooper
Education Consultant
State Department of Education

MINNESOTA
Richard Clark
Science Specialist
State Department of Education

MISSISSIPPI
Jack Lynch
Director of Public Relations
State Department of Education

MISSOURI
Warren Solomon
Curriculum Consultant
Department of Elementary
   and Secondary Education

MONTANA
Ed Berquist
Special Assistant to the
   Superintendent
State Office of Public Instruction

NEBRASKA
Deborah Romanek
Math Consultant
State Department of Education

NEVADA
Pat Boyd
Director of Basic Education
State Department of Education

NEW HAMPSHIRE
Susan Rowe
Curriculm Supervisor
Migrant Education Program
State Department Of Education

NEW JERSEY
Bill Mancuso
County Superintendent of Schools
State Department of Education

NEW MEXICO
Claire Fenton
Math Specialist
State Department of Education

NEW YORK
Susan Agruso
Associate in Science Education
State Education Department

NORTH CAROLINA
Grace Drain
Coordinator, Teacher Recruitment
   Office
State Department of Public
   Instruction

NORTH DAKOTA
Chuck DeRemer
Director of Educational Support
   Services
State Department of Public
   Instruction

OHIO
Pat Huston
Communications Consultant
State Department of Education

OKLAHOMA
Doris K. Grigsby, Ed.D.
Science Specialist
State Department of Education

OREGON
Ray Thiess
Science Coordinator
State Department of Education

PENNSYLVANIA
John McDermott
Senior Science Director
State Department of Education

PUERTO RICO
Julio Lopez Ferrao
Director of Science Program
Department of Education

RHODE ISLAND
Lorraine Webber
Special Assistant to the
   Commissioner
State Department of Education

SOUTH CAROLINA
Lonnie Craven
Accreditation Supervisor
State Department of Education

SOUTH DAKOTA
Judy Bassett
Elementary Curriculm Specialist
Department of Education and
   Cultural Affairs

TENNESSEE
John Gaines
Director of Secondary Education
State Department of Education

TEXAS
Barbara Ten Brink
Science Education Specialist
Texas Education Agency

UTAH
LaMar Allred
Specialist, Science Education
State Office of Education

VERMONT
Gail Breslauer
Consultant
State Department of Education

VIRGINIA
Joseph Exline, Ph.D.
Associate Director for Science
State Department of Education

VIRGIN ISLANDS
Rosa White
Science Coordinator
Department of Education

WASHINGTON
David Kennedy
Program Administrator for
   Curriculum
State Department of Public
   Instruction

WEST VIRGINIA
Barbara Jones, Ph.D.
Coordinator, Science and Social
   Studies
State Department of Education

WISCONSIN
Harlene Ames
Educational Consultant
State Department of Public
   Instruction

WYOMING
Alan G. Wheeler
Assistant Superintendent
State Department of Education

Appendix C

State-Level Winners

Listed below are the Division 1 and Division 2 coordinators whose teams won their state Orbiter-Naming Program competitions and the ship's name chosen by their teams.

STATE	DIVISION 1	DIVISION 2
Alabama	*Eagle* Pamela Sayre Clements High School Athens	*Victoria* Sophia Clifford Erwin High School Birmingham
Alaska	*Resolution* Richard Smith Birchwood ABC Elementary School Eagle River	*Resolution* Joyce Ower East Anchorage High School Anchorage
American Samoa	*Meteor* Eline Maino Matafao Elementary School Pago Pago	*Hōkūle'a* Paul E. Cassens Tafuna High School Pago Pago
Arizona	*Endeavour* Cathleen A. Brown Four Peaks School Fountain Hills	*Victoria* Patty Grossman Desert Sky Junior High Glendale
Arkansas	*Calypso* Gail Thomas Daniel Middle School Crosset	*Endeavour* M. Beth Greenway Parkview Arts Magnet School Little Rock
Bureau of Indian Affairs	*Victoria* James White Crystal Boarding School Navajo, NM	
California	*Adventure* Scott Stark Mesa View School Huntington Beach	*Phoenix* Penny Moore Piedmont High School Piedmont
Colorado	*Endeavour* Joan K. Zack Abner Baker Elementary School Fort Morgan	*Endeavour* Bradley K. Loucks Bookcliff Middle School Grand Junction
Connecticut	*Endeavour* Rosemary I. Payne A.H. Rockwell Elementary School Bethel	*Nautilus* Robert W. Mellette Betsy Ross Arts Magnet School New Haven

Delaware	*Phoenix* Cynthia L. Pochomis Richardson Park Learning Center Wilmington	*Nautilus* Melinda Thornton Laurel Middle School Laurel
Department of Defense Dependents Schools	*Resolution* Patricia Bryan Boeblingen Elementary School (Germany)	*Resolution* Jeanneatte Alfe Croughton Middle School (England)
Department of State Overseas Schools	*Trieste* Vivian Lim International School, Manila Philippines	*Endeavour* Karen Pearson Taipei American School Taiwan
District of Columbia	*Victoria* Connie Cowley Alexander R. Shepard Elementary School	
Florida	*Endeavour* Patricia O'Dor Lockhart Elementary School Orlando	*Victory* Helene Monagle Mesa Ponce de Leon Middle School Coral Gables
Georgia	*Phoenix* Marilyn Allen Big Shanty Elementary School Kennesaw	*Endeavour* Martha K. Cantrell Tallulah Falls School, Inc. Tallulah Falls
Guam		*Phoenix* Jul Hoehl Notre Dame High School Tolofofo
Hawaii	*Resolution* Marie Ann Kohara Pearl Ridge Elementary School Aiea	*Nautilus* Sandra Larson Hawaii Preparatory Academy Kamuela
Idaho	*Endeavor* Stephanie Murphy McCall-Connelly Elementary School McCall	*Horizon* Steven D. Branting Jenifer Junior High School Lewiston
Illinois	*Endeavor* Mary Caldwell Coultrap Middle School Geneva	*Endeavour* William E. Glennon Kimball Middle School Elgin
Indiana	*Endeavor* Barbara Brewer Arcola Elementary School Arcola	*Desire* David A. Kahn Boone Grove Jr./Sr. High School Boone Grove

Iowa	*Endeavour*	*Endeavor*
	Susan Kallestad	Mary Frank
	Pomeroy Community School	Spencer Middle School
	Pomeroy	Spencer

Kansas	*Victoria*	*Endeavor*
	Julia Wood	Eric Flescher
	Kensler School	Shawnee Mission West High School
	Wichita	Shawnee Mission

Kentucky	*Victoria*	*Resolution*
	Cindy A. Ellis	Marlene Coursey
	Chenoweth Elementary School	Caldwell County Middle School
	Louisville	Princeton

Louisiana	*Victoria*	*Endeavour*
	John Swang	Sandra Leder
	Mandeville Middle School	Forrest K. White Middle School
	Mandeville	Lake Charles

Maine	*Endeavour*	*Griffin*
	Lillian Castonguay	James Henry
	Martel School	Penobscot Community Elementary School
	Lewiston	Penobscot

Maryland	*Dove*	*Endeavour*
	Elizabeth M. Burley	Robert Handy
	Homestead-Wakefield Elementary School	Fallston High School
	Bel Air	Fallston

Massachusetts	*Endeavour*	*Victory*
	Kristine Gustafson	Marie J. Neal
	Walter J. Paton School	Ottoson Junior High School
	Shrewsbury	Arlington

Michigan	*Victoria*	*Horizon*
	Richard Thibault	Kaarin McColl
	R. J. Steeby Elementary School	Bloomfield Hills Middle School
	Wayland	Bloomfield Hills

Minnesota	*Endeavor*	*Calypso*
	Joyce Wiebusch	Mary Jo Aiken
	Janesville Elementary School	Benilde-St. Margaret's High School
	Janesville	St. Louis Park

Mississippi	*Endeavour*	*Endeavour*
	Martha S. Riales	Rebecca Becnel
	Senatobia Middle School	Long Beach High School
	Senatobia	Long Beach

Missouri	*Adventure*	*Resolution*
	Rose Diane Warren	Linda Kralina
	Clinton County R-III, Ellis Elementary School	Hazelwood Central Senior High School
	Plattsburg	Florissant

Montana	*Resolution* Joan Kuchel Russell Elementary School Missoula	*Phoenix* Paul L. Dorrance Helena High School Helena
Nebraska	*Endeavor* Patricia Garton Central Elementary School Fairbury	*Horizon* Mark Urwiller Kearney Senior High School Kearney
Nevada	*Investigator* JoAnn Elston Echo Loder Elementary School Reno	*Resolution* Bob Tye Archie Clayton Middle School Reno
New Hampshire	*Calypso* Daniel D. Cherry Towle Elementary School Newport	*Polar Star* George Drinkwater Dover Junior High School Dover
New Jersey	*Nautilus* Maxine Cahn James Madison Intermediate School Edison	*Calypso* Mary Ann Haug Newton High School Newton
New Mexico	*Victory* Sylvia A. Fox Kennedy Middle School Albuquerque	*Endeavour* Janis St. Louis Zia Intermediate School Artesia
New York	*Endeavor* Deborah Leff Walt Whitman Elementary School Woodbury	*Resolution* Allen L. Kurtz J.H.S. 118X/William W. Niles/ P.A.C.E. Academy Bronx
North Carolina	*North Star* Cynthia Jones East Iredell Elementary School Statesville	*Calypso* Gayle Morgan North Duplin Jr./Sr. High School Calypso
North Dakota	*Endeavour* Elynn Severson Hawthorne Elementary School Fargo	*Victoria* Rebecca Jungemann Wolford Public School Wolford
Ohio	*Resolution* Mary Eve Corrigan The Columbus Academy Gahanna	*Victoria* David Eric Hanson Alliance High School Alliance
Oklahoma	*Endeavor* Janet Beggerly Wilson Elementary School Miami	*Rising Star* Debbie Jensen Woodward Junior High School Woodward

Oregon	*Pathfinder*	*Victory*
	Mrs. Wes A. Brown	Jodi Johnson
	Churchill Elementary School	Cascade Junior High School
	Baker	Bend
Pennsylvania	*Blake*	*Endeavour*
	Robert Boehmer	Geraldine McFarland
	Schnecksville Elementary School	Schenley High School Teacher Center
	Schnecksville	Pittsburgh
Puerto Rico	*Royal Tern*	*Victoria*
	Joan Zenteno	Francisco Rodriguez
	Caribbean School	Immaculate Conception Academy
	Ponce	Mayaguez
Rhode Island	*Horizon*	*Nautilus*
	Marilyn I. Remick	John McDevitt
	Western Hills Elementary School	Joseph H. Gaudet Middle School
	Cranston	Middletown
South Carolina	*Endeavor*	*Endeavour*
	Margaret Smith	Cathy S. Scott
	Chesterfield Middle School	Lexington High School
	Chesterfield	Lexington
South Dakota	*Endeavor*	*Calypso*
	Dorothy Piper	Anita Miller
	Wood Elementary School	St. Elizabeth Seton School
	Wood	Rapid City
Tennessee	*Phoenix*	*Godspeed*
	Margaret V. Dalimonte	Donna A. Berry
	Cedar Bluff Intermediate School	Baylor School
	Knoxville	Chattanooga
Texas	*Endurance*	*Endeavor*
	Fredia Hester	Robert Norman
	East Side Elementary School	Irvin High School
	Palacios	El Paso
Utah	*Victory*	*Nautilus*
	Virginia B. Cate	Robinette Bowden
	Kaysville Elementary School	Central Davis Junior High
	Kaysville	Layton
Vermont	*Trieste*	
	Kurt A. Sherman	
	Westford Elementary School	
	Westford	
Virginia	*Godspeed*	*Adventure*
	Amy Steward	Ann Bordwine
	Spring Hill Elementary School	Northwood High School
	McLean	Saltville

Virgin Islands		*R/V Gulf Stream* Ann Marie Gibbs Elena L. Christian Junior High School Christiansted, St. Croix
Washington	*Deepstar* Jacqueline E. Lyons Robert Reid Elementary School Cheney	*Chatham* Leslie R. Hastings Stevenson High School Stevenson
West Virginia	*Godspeed* Marsha C. Bailes Summersville Gifted Resource Center Summersville	*Deepstar* Diane M. Berdar Paden City Middle School Paden City
Wisconsin	*Calypso* Alyce J. Wehrenberg Hamilton Elementary School La Crosse	*Adventure* Timothy Milligan St. Mary's Springs High School Fond du Lac
Wyoming	*Resolution* Patsy B. Bailey Northside Elementary School Lander	*Nautilus* Larry Dwayne Adams Cheyenne East High School Cheyenne

Appendix D

Names Proposed for OV-105

The 422 names of ships proposed for OV-105 are listed in alphabetical order. If more than one team suggested a name, the frequency is noted in parentheses.

Admiral
Advance (4)
Adventure (308)
Adventure Galley
Adventures
Adventuress
Air Dragon
Albacore
Albatross (15)
Alcyone (2)
Alert (2)
All American (2)
Alliance (26)
Aluminaut (14)
Alvin (33)
America (14)
America Liberty
American
American Clipper
American Eagle
American Spirit
Amerigo
Angel
Archangel
Archimedes (4)
Arcturus
Argo (27)
Argonaut (10)
Ariel (2)
Arizona
Ark (3)
Assistante
Astrea
Astrolabe (10)
Atlantis
Audacity
Aurora (15)
Auxiliary
Avenger
Bald Eagle (2)
Beacon (4)

Beagle (41)
Bear
Beluga
Ben Franklin (10)
Betsy Ross
Black Foot
Black Hawk
Blake
Blossom
Bonaventure
Bonhomme Richard (3)
Bounty (7)
Brendan (4)
Bright Star
Californian
Calypso (366)
Canmar Explorer
Cape Columbia
Caravel
Celestia
Centaurian
Centennial
Centurion (6)
Challenger (2)
Challenger 2
Challenger 7
Champion (3)
Chance
Chantier
Chatham
Clermont (15)
Climax
Clio
Clipper (2)
Comet (11)
Concepcion (3)
Conception (6)
Concord
Condor
Conqueror (4)
Conquest (5)

Conrad
Conshelf III
Consolation
Constellation (71)
Constitution (140)
Contender
Contest
Courageous
Cruiser
Crusader (4)
Cutty Sark
Cyclops
DS-2
Dauntless
Dauphine
Dawn Star
Deep Diver
Deep Quest (23)
Deepstar (101)
Defender
Defiance (5)
Deliverance
Desire (5)
Destiny (3)
Dias
Diligence (2)
Diving Saucer
Dolphin (9)
Dove (15)
Dragon Ship
Dreadnought (4)
Dubuque
Eagle (44)
Eagle Wing (3)
Eastward
Echo
Eclipse
Emigrant
Encounter
Endeavor (22)
Endeavour (1016)

Endurance (82)
Enterprise (29)
Erebus (3)
Esperanza
Essex (9)
Eureka (4)
Evergreen
Excalibur (5)
Excel
Expedition
Experiment (5)
Explorer (17)
Faith
Falcon (6)
Fearless (2)
Fire Fly
Flip (2)
Flyer
Flying Cloud (106)
Flying Mist
Forward
Fox
Fram (4)
Freedom (3)
Friendship (2)
Frontier
Fulton
Fury (2)
Gabriel (5)
Galathea (4)
Galaxy
Galaxy Explorer
Gallaica
Galleon (5)
Genesis Ark
Gettysburg
Gift of God
Gjoa
Gloire
Glomar Challenger (4)
Glory (2)

Godspeed (72)
Golden Eagle
Golden Hind (17)
Good Hope
Goodspeed (13)
Grande Hermine
Great Eastern (2)
Great Republic (3)
Great Western
Greek Tribune
Greenpeace
Griffin (24)
Gulf Stream (5)
Half Moon (209)
Hamilton
Hannah
Hero (44)
High Point
Hokule'a (5)
Hope (23)
Hopewell (48)
Horizon (33)
Hornet
Humbolt
II Core
Imperial Eagle
Independence (18)
Intrepid (21)
Investigator (38)
Invincible (6)
Itasca
Jamestown
Jason, Jr.
Kennedy (5)
Kingsport (2)
Kitty Hawk (4)
Knickerbocker
Knorr (2)
Kon-Tiki (22)
Langley (2)
Leader
Lexington
Liberty (26)
Lightning (20)
Link
Lisbon
Long Serpent
Los Indios
Magellica
Majestic (3)
Manitowoc

Marquette
Matthew (7)
Mayflower (84)
McAuliffe
McAuliffe VII
Memory
Mercury
Merrimac (2)
Messenger
Metacomet
Meteor (17)
Midway
Mimi (4)
Minden
Missoli
Monarch
Monitor (18)
Moonraker
Morgan
Morning
Morning Star (2)
Mystic
N.E.M.O.
N.O.A.A.
Nautilus (391)
Navigator (6)
Neeskay
Nekton
Nemo
Nero
New Horizon (7)
New World (2)
Niagara (3)
Nightengale (2)
Nimitz (3)
Nina (22)
Norma
Norge (2)
North Star (11)
Northern Light
Northern Star (2)
Northwind (4)
Nova
Oceanus
Octorara
Odyssey (17)
Old Ironsides (2)
Olympia (21)
Olympic (3)
Onward
Orion (7)

Osberg
Otto
PX-15
Pathfinder (7)
Patience
Patriot
Peaceland
Peacemaker (2)
Pegasus (5)
Pelican (3)
Peral
Perseverance (2)
Phoenix (198)
Photos
Pilgrim
Pinta (15)
Pioneer (9)
Pisces (5)
Pizzaro
Polar Star (2)
Polaris (7)
Porpoise
Poseidon II
Prevail
Pride
Prometheus (2)
Prospector (3)
Protector (2)
Qayao Ayagatuli
Quest (17)
Quintain
Ra II (3)
Rainbow (13)
Ranger (8)
Ready
Recovery (2)
Red Eye Wolf
Red White & Blue
Redstone
Regina Maris
Relentless
Reliance (5)
Reprisal
Rescue
Research (4)
Resolute
Resolution (367)
Restless
Resurgam
Revenge (5)
Revolution

Rising Star (14)
Rocket Tosser
Roosevelt (22)
Royal S.C.
Royal Tern
Santa Clara
Santa Maria (68)
Santiago (2)
Saratoga
Savannah (66)
Scorpion
Scout
Sea Dragon
Sea Gull
Sea Witch (2)
Searcher (2)
Searchthrift
Sequoia
Serapis (2)
Shamrock
Shangri-La
Sirius (22)
Skylark
Solace
Sovereign
Space Link
Speedwell (5)
Spirit
Star (2)
Star Bound
Star Flight
Star I (2)
Star III (3)
Star of Gladness
Star of Life
Stardrift
Stark (2)
Starling (3)
Stars and Stripes (9)
Stellar Eagle
Stingray
Success (2)
Sunbird
Super Sonic
Supply
Surveyor (2)
Survivor
Swallow
Tech-Diver
Tektite II
Tenacity

Terra Nova (23)
Terror
Thresher (2)
Tiger
Tigris (4)
Titanic (2)
Topaz
Tradewind
Tranquility
Travailleur
Traveller
Trident
Trieste (57)
Trinidad (17)

Triton (29)
Triumph (7)
Twilight (3)
U.S.A. #1
United States (5)
Unitie (3)
Unity (6)
Uranie
Utopia (2)
Valiant (4)
Vanguard (2)
Vasa
Vega (13)
Vema (5)

Venture (3)
Victoria (584)
Victorious
Victory (142)
Viking (5)
Vincennes (7)
Virginia (2)
Vision (3)
Vittoria
Voyager
Vulcan (4)
Wager
Wanderer
Warrior

Washington (4)
Wasp
Welcome (2)
West Wind
Westward (2)
White Star (2)
Windward (11)
Wyatt Earp
Yankee (2)
Young America (8)
Youth Shuttle
Zenith

A piece of the ship **Endeavour** *presented to NASA by the University of Rhode Island's Graduate School of Oceanography at the rollout ceremony of the orbiter* **Endeavour.**

Appendix E

Endeavour, Ship and Shuttle

His Majesty's Bark *Endeavour*

When the Lords of the Admiralty and The Royal Society agreed to sponsor a joint voyage of exploration to the South Pacific in 1768, the Royal Navy purchased a Whitby-built collier, *Earl of Pembroke,* to make the journey and chose Lieutenant James Cook to command it.

The colliers were sturdy ships, flat-bottomed with bluff bows, and broad-beamed, to carry large cargoes in the North Sea coal trade. Renamed *Endeavour,* Cook's small ship (length, 97 ft, 8 in [29.6m]; beam, 29 ft, 2 in [8.8m]; depth of hold, 15 ft, 4 in [4.6m]; 366 tons [329.4 metric tons]) also was refitted. When it set sail in August 1768, *Endeavour* carried extra sails and rigging; carpenter and blacksmith shops; food, including livestock for fresh meat; guns and ammunition; medical equipment; delicate scientific instruments; a variety of artist's supplies; and "trifles and tringits" for trading.

Cook, known as an experienced and able seaman, navigator, cartographer, and amateur astronomer captained a complement of 93 men, including crew, marines, and 11 scientists and artists with their servants. He left England with specific objectives: For the Royal Society, to observe the Transit of Venus at Tahiti, June 3, 1769; for the Admiralty, under secret orders, to seek the Great Southern Continent thought to exist in the southern hemisphere and to chart the coast of New Zealand and any lands discovered.

After completing the astronomical observations, Cook sailed southwest. He found no southern continent, but circumnavigated New Zealand and proved it was two islands. Continuing westward, Cook reached the southeast coast of New Holland (Australia). Following the coast north, he named Botany Bay for the abundance of vegetation and specimens found there, and the Endeavour River for the place where his ship ran aground. It was through this event that Cook discovered the Great Barrier Reef. En route back to England, Cook rounded the northern coast of Australia and confirmed that the continent was separate from islands in the north.

Cook made one voyage in *Endeavour.* His achievements were many and impressive and set standards for those who followed. He crossed the South Pacific as no one had before him; his surveying and charting produced extremely accurate maps of New Zealand and the east coast of Australia; and the recorded astronomical and hydrographical data were invaluable. He also was the first to take scientists and artists to observe, examine, and record plants and animals, to collect specimens, and to illustrate their findings.

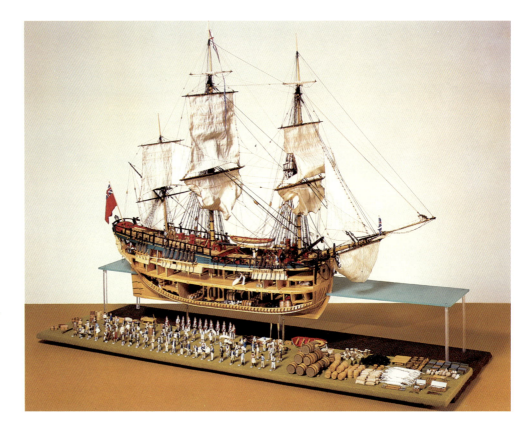

*The model depicts **Endeavour** at 1:00 upon the afternoon of Friday, 26 August 1768, one hour before sailing from Plymouth with 94 persons on board. Courtesy of National Maritime Museum, Greenwich, London.*

*Crew for the first flight of the orbiter **Endeavour** (from left to right)—Mission Specialists Kathryn Thornton, Bruce Melnick, and Pierre Thout, Commander Daniel Brandenstein, Pilot Kevin Chilton, Mission Specialists Thomas Akers and Richard Hieb. NASA photo.*

'Through the thousands of specimens of new plant species, innumerable sketches and paintings of wildlife, and portraits of natives, he enriched European knowledge of the Pacific. And he set a precedent. Teams of scientists and artists became accepted members of ships' crews, and with their chemicals, containers for specimens, and artists' equipment, the ships of exploration that followed Cook came to be described as "floating laboratories."

Cook's immediate recognition came from his contributions to the health of men at sea. A prevention and cure for scurvy had been published several years earlier, and Cook tested the suggested diet and health regimens on the *Endeavour* voyage. He experimented with citrus and other fruits, sauerkraut, onions, grasses, and fresh food when possible. He enforced cleanliness in both personal hygiene and the ship's environment. He endorsed exercise whenever they were near land. Men were lost by accidents and other illnesses, but not one from scurvy.

Cook returned to England in July 1771. He was promoted to commander, and a year later returned to the South Pacific with two ships.

Of *Endeavour,* Cook said, "A better ship for such a service I never would wish for." After 1771, *Endeavour* saw service in the Falkland Islands and perhaps in the North Sea before being sold to the French. In the 1790s, she ran aground on a reef off Newport, Rhode Island. The University of Rhode Island's Graduate School of Oceanography has a sternpost remnant of Cook's *Endeavour.* At the rollout ceremony of the orbiter *Endeavour,* the School presented NASA with a piece of the original ship. The artifact will be carried aboard the orbiter *Endeavour's* first voyage.

Orbiter Vehicle (OV) 105 *Endeavour*

In April 1983, under contract to NASA, Rockwell International's Space Transportation Systems Division, Downey, California, began the construction of a structural spare orbiter for completion in 1988. The structural spare is a structural shell, no systems installation or parts.

The $400 million structural spares program included the upper and lower forward fuselage, crew compartment, nose, landing gear doors, forward reaction control system, airlock, and aft fuselage, which were constructed at Rockwell's Downey facility. The payload bay doors were built by Rockwell in Tulsa, Oklahoma, and its Columbus, Ohio, Division constructed the body flap.

General Dynamics' Convair Aerospace Division, San Diego, California, built the mid fuselage structural spare. Grumman Corporation, Bethpage, New York, constructed the wings, including elevons and main landing gear doors. Fairchild Republic, Farmingdale, Long Island, New York, provided the vertical stabilizer and rudder/speed brake. The orbital maneuvering system/reaction control system pods were built by McDonnell Douglas Astronautics Company, St. Louis, Missouri.

On August 1, 1987, NASA awarded Rockwell a $1.3 billion contract to build a replacement orbiter using the structural spares. The orbiter, designated OV-105, was assembled at Rockwell's facility in Palmdale, California. In May 1989, with the announcement of the winners of the NASA Orbiter-Naming competition, OV-105 received its name *Endeavour*.

Endeavour was delivered to NASA on April 25, 1991. Essentially identical to its sister ships, *Columbia, Discovery,* and *Atlantis, Endeavour* is distinguished from them by two main differences: a drag chute to aid deceleration and reduce loads on the landing gear and brakes, and design features that may later accommodate extended orbits of up to 28 days. There are also a carbon braking system, a quick-release escape hatch, and nose-wheel steering.

Endeavour is capable of flying 100 missions. It weighs approximately 68,000 kilograms (150,000 lbs) (without the main engines) and measures 38 meters (125 ft) in length with a wingspan of about 24 meters (78 ft). The payload bay is 18.3 meters (60 ft) long and 4.6 meters (15 ft) in diameter.

Endeavour's first launch, Space Shuttle Mission STS-49, is scheduled for spring 1992. The Commander is Daniel C. Brandenstein, Capt., USN, with Kevin P. Chilton, Major, USAF, Pilot. Mission Specialists are Pierre J. Thuot, Cdr., USN; Kathryn C. Thorton, Ph.D.; Richard J. Hieb; Thomas D. Akers, Major, USAF; and Bruce E. Melnick, Cdr., USCG.

The crew will attach a new booster and redeploy the *Intelsat* satellite. In addition, three spacewalks will be performed in an extensive test of techniques to be employed during assembly of Space Station *Freedom*. *Endeavour* is slated for the first element launch of *Freedom* in March 1995.

The STS-49 Mission patch, designed by its crewmembers, captures the spirit of exploration which originated with the early seagoing vessels. The ship is H. M. Bark Endeavour, commanded by James Cook on his first scientific expedition. On the Shuttle Endeavour's first flight, the crew will expand the horizons of space operations, just as Cook set new ideals for exploration during his voyage.

The flags flying on Endeavour's masts bear the colors of the two schools that won the competition to name the new orbiter: the blue and gold of Senatobia Middle School, Mississippi, and the green and white of Tallulah Falls School, Inc., Georgia.

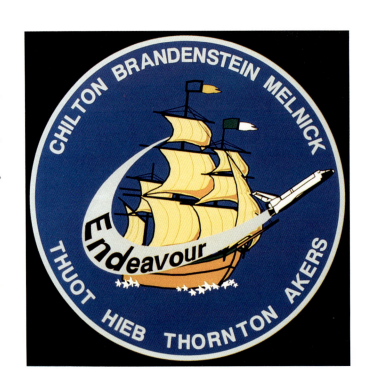

NASA Education Offices

Publication lists, films lists, and information about other services, including the Teacher Resource Center Network, are available from the education offices at the NASA field centers. Listed below are the centers and the states they serve.

NASA Ames Research Center
Moffett Field, CA 94035
  Serves Alaska, Arizona, California, Hawaii, Idaho, Montana, Nevada, Oregon, Utah, Washington, and Wyoming.

NASA Goddard Space Flight Center
Greenbelt, MD 20771
  Serves Connecticut, Delaware, District of Columbia, Maine, Maryland, Massachusetts, New Hampshire, New Jersey, New York, Pennsylvania, Rhode Island, and Vermont.

NASA Jet Propulsion Laboratory
4800 Oak Grove Drive
Pasadena, CA 91109
  Serves inquires related to space exploration and other JPL activities.

NASA Lyndon B. Johnson Space Center
Houston, TX 77058
  Serves Colorado, Kansas, Nebraska, New Mexico, North Dakota, Oklahoma, South Dakota, and Texas.

NASA John F. Kennedy Space Center
Kennedy Space Center, FL 32899
  Serves Florida, Georgia, Puerto Rico, and the Virgin Islands.

NASA Langley Research Center
Hampton, VA 23665
  Serves Kentucky, North Carolina, South Carolina, Virginia, and West Virginia.

NASA Lewis Research Center
Cleveland, OH 44135
  Serves Illinois, Indiana, Michigan, Minnesota, Ohio, and Wisconsin.

NASA George C. Marshall Space Flight Center
Marshall Space Flight Center, AL 35812
  Serves Alabama, Arkansas, Iowa, Louisiana, Missouri, and Tennessee.

NASA John C. Stennis Space Center
Stennis Space Center, MS 39529
  Serves Mississippi.

For more information about audio visual materials, contact:
NASA CORE
Lorrain County Joint Vocational School
15181 Route 58 South
Oberlin, OH 44074

Acknowledgments

NASA is grateful to the following individuals (identified with the offices or positions they held at the time) and organizations who assisted with the Orbiter-Naming Program (1988-1989) and the preparation of this publication (1990-1991).

Orbiter-Naming Program

NASA Headquarters

Dr. Robert W. Brown
Director, Educational Affairs Division

Frank C. Owens
Deputy Director, Educational Affairs Division

Dr. Eddie Anderson
Chief, Elementary and Secondary Programs Branch

Muriel M. Thorne
Manager, Orbiter-Naming Program Elementary and Secondary Programs Branch

Larry B. Bilbrough
Deborah J. Rivera
Elementary and Secondary Programs Branch

Pamela M. Bacon
Cheryl A. Manning
NASA Teacher in Space Program Oklahoma State University

Gloria A. Barnes
Editorial Assistant Educational Publications and Special Services Branch

Julia D. Meredith
Legislative Affairs Specialist

Teresa G. Sindelar
Public Information Officer for Education

Jeffrey P. Petrino
Contracting Officer Contracts and Grants Division

Evelyn L. Thames
Tawana M. Clary
Astronaut Appearances and Speakers Services Special Events Branch

NASA Centers

Garth A. Hull, *Chief*
Thomas B. Clausen
Educational Programs Office Ames Research Center

Elva Bailey, Chief
Richard N. Crone
Educational Programs Goddard Space Flight Center

James D. Poindexter
Educational Specialist Johnson Space Center

Raymond R. Corey, Chief
June Buchanan
Education and Awareness Branch Kennedy Space Center

Roger A. Hathaway
Education and Information Specialist Langley Research Center

Dr. R. Lynn Bondurant, Jr., Chief
Anita Solarz
Educational Services Office Lewis Research Center

Jeffrey Ehmen
Public Services and Education Branch Marshall Space Flight Center

Dr. Jerry Brown
Education Specialist Stennis Space Center

Council of Chief State School Officers

Gordon M. Ambach
Executive Director

Dr. Donna H. Schoeny
Project Director

Tommie Williams
Project Associate

William Shepardson
Project Assistant

189

Task Force

American Association for Counseling and Development

American Association of School Administrators

American Federation of Teachers

Challenger Center for Space Science Education

District of Columbia Public Schools

International Reading Association

National Association of Elementary School Principals

National Association of Secondary School Principals

National Catholic Education Association

National Education Association

National School Boards Association

Prince George's County Public Schools

San Antonio Public Schools

Young Astronaut Council

Educational Affairs Division, NASA Headquarters

NASA Aerospace Education Services Project, Oklahoma State University

Council of Chief State School Officers

National Air and Space Museum

Ted A. Maxwell
Chairman, Center for Earth and Planetary Studies

Kasse Andrews-Weller
Chief, Office of Education

Janet O'Donnell
Carolyn E. Schmidt
Education Specialists

National Judges

NAMES COMMITTEE

NASA Headquarters

Robert L. Crippen, Chair
Barbara E. Selby
Leonard B. Sirota
Office of Space Flight

Dr. Sylvia D. Fries
Frank C. Owens
Kenneth S. Pedersen
Muriel M. Thorne
Office of External Relations

Joseph K. Alexander
Office of Space Flight and Applications

PROJECTS COMMITTEE

NASA Headquarters

Dr. Eddie Anderson
Charles P. Boyle
Dr. Sylvia D. Fries
Muriel M. Thorne, Chair
Office of External Relations

Pamela M. Bacon
NASA Teacher in Space Program
Dr. Harry B. Herzer III
Dr. James Gregory Marlins
Gregory L. Vogt
NASA Aerospace Education Services Project Oklahoma State University

Dr. Bevan French
Charles Redmond
Office of Space Science and Applications

Dr. John-David Bartoe
Office of Space Station

NASA Centers

Eugene Hudson
Educational Programs Goddard Space Flight Center

Marchelle D. Canright
Roger A. Hathaway
Education and Information Specialists Langley Research Center

Dr. R. Lynn Bondurant, Jr.
Educational Services Office Lewis Research Center

From Ship to Shuttle

NASA Headquarters

Muriel M. Thorne
Editor
Elementary and Secondary Programs Branch

Naomi C. Ford
Dr. Harry B. Herzer III
NASA Aerospace Education Services Program
Oklahoma State University

Beryle L. Byrd
Printing and Graphics Branch

Althea R. Washington
Broadcast and Audio Visual Branch

Bill Ingalls
EVCO Productions

Karlisa L. Smith
Colleen E. White
Elementary and Secondary Programs Branch

Howard S. Golden
Chief, Educational Publications and Special Services

Adrianne Onderdonk Dudden
Graphic Design

The Space Shuttle orbiter Endeavour atop NASA's Shuttle Carrier Aircraft approaching touchdown at Ellington Field near the Johnson Space Center (TX) during its transport from Rockwell International in Palmdale, California, to Kennedy Space Center (FL). NASA photo.